Over 70
and I Don't Mean MPH

Other books by Marilyn Reynolds

Shut Up!

No More Sad Goodbyes

Love Rules

If You Loved Me

Baby Help

Too Soon For Jeff

Detour for Emmy

Telling

Beyond Dreams

But What About Me?

I Won't Read and You Can't Make Me:
Reaching Reluctant Teen Readers

Over 70
and I Don't Mean MPH

Reflections on the Gifts of Longevity

By Marilyn Reynolds

Morning Glory Press

Buena Park, California

Marilyn Reynolds

ISBN 978-0-9844283-4-2
0-9844283-4-8

Library of Congress Cataloging-in-Publication Data available upon request.

MORNING GLORY PRESS, INC.
6595 San Haroldo Way   Buena Park, CA 90620-3748
714.828.1998, 1.888.612.8254   FAX 714.828.2049
e-mail: info@morningglorypress.com
Web site: www.morningglorypress.com
Printed and bound in the United States of America

Contents

Acknowledgments

For early and late draft readings, insights and encourage-
ment, and general help along the way, I am ever grateful to
Dale Dodson, Marg Dodson, Kathy Harvey, Karen Kasaba,
Judy Laird, Barbara Lazar, Kathy Riskin Orihuela, Rodolfo
Orihuela, Sharon Reynolds Kyle, Matthew Reynolds, Leesa
Phaneuf Reynolds, Marilyn Sandbom, Bill Schmidt, and
Jeannie Ward.

A heartfelt thank you to Jeanne Warren Lindsay for going
the extra mile.

Cast
of Mostly Recurring Characters

Dale Dodson, brother

Margaret Dodson, Dale's wife, my sister-in-law

Cindi Foncannon, daughter

Ashley DiFalco, Cindi's daughter, my granddaughter

Kerry Foncannon, Cindi's son, my grandson

Matthew Reynolds, son

Leesa Phaneuf Reynolds, Matt's wife, my daughter-in-law

Mika, Matt and Leesa's daughter, my granddaughter

Michael Reynolds, husband

Sharon Reynolds-Kyle, daughter

Doug Kyle, Sharon's husband, my son-in-law

Subei and Lena, Sharon and Doug's daughters,
      my granddaughters

Sunny Merritt, slighter larger than miniature Schnauzer
      in residence

In a Category All Her Own

Mimi Avocada, my own personal Grand Goddess of the Harmonic Universe, who revealed herself to me during a time of significant stress. If you simply can't wait for a more complete explanation, jump ahead to page 103.

Life is a shipwreck
but we must not forget to sing in the lifeboats.
Voltaire, *Candide*

Preface

When I first set out to write this, I saw it as a light-hearted look at moving from the "middle-age" category to the "old-age" category — a personal accounting, but also a recognition of concerns and experiences common to most at this stage of life. I would not deny the travails of old age, or put too light a spin on the inevitable deterioration and death that waits around some not too distant corner, but I would also, mainly, bask in the joy of having become old in a way that had not been within the reach of our grandparents or even our parents.

In addition to being insightful and entertaining (words I hoped to read from reviewers) I also saw it as something of an example for the Baby Boomers who are still mostly reeling in disbelief that the oldest of them have now reached the dreaded senior citizen category. I watch them watching me, these half-generation younger friends, comparing my seventies to their parents' seventies, and I know that my example shines a ray of hope onto the unreasonable fear of aging they've held since first realizing that they, too, would reach the over-thirty age of untrustworthiness.

The intended consistently light tone, with just a sprinkling of the unavoidable poignancy that comes from knowing the end is relatively near, took a turn when it became increasingly obvious that my husband Mike's difficulties tracking the details of everyday life were more than his "artist's personality" could account for. In July of 2009, shortly after his 69th birthday, Mike was diagnosed with Frontotemporal Dementia (FTD), a lesser-known form of dementia than Alzheimer's, but equally devastating. My husband and partner of forty-one years soon lost his capacity to function independently and I fell into the role of caregiver, a role we're hearing more and more about these days.

At first I tried to include in this work-in-progress examples of the daily heartbreaks and challenges of life with an FTD partner. To ignore the burden of caregiving in this middle-old time smacked of a Pollyannaish dishonesty. But even though my *life* included the humor, joys, and ironies of aging, along with the depth of sorrow and loss that came with Mike's rapid and devastating deterioration, try as I might I simply could not include both sides of my life, here, in this one book, in a way that did justice to either side.

The ongoing story of Mike's shift from a bright, funny, talented man to a volatile, barely verbal, helpless shell of himself is for the next book. If you're in a hurry for those details you can find them on my blog at www.friendsofmikes.com.

In the meantime, what follows is in keeping with my original intention, reflections on the mostly lighter side of aging, coupled with the recognition that nothing lasts.

Marilyn Reynolds
December 2011

On Approaching Seventy
September 2004

A year from now I'll hit the seventy mark. I've been in the category of "young-old" for the past five years and at seventy I'll go up a category to "middle-old." Seventy brings with it a certain drama, and it's got me thinking of my own mortality in ways that are much less abstract than they once were. I'm also noticing in myself, and in other young-old friends, a tendency to contemplate the lives of those that came before us. I drag out pictures of my mother at seventy and take heart that I don't look nearly as old as she did then. Maybe that's a sign that I *won't* be hit by a stroke at the age of seventy-eight as was she — that I won't slip into the dementia that ultimately left her sitting immobilized in her wheel chair, knowing nothing of the people or the world around her.

From this nearly seventy perspective, thoughts of my grandmother take on a different hue. Where I once thought of her mostly in relation to myself, simply as my Granny, I now try to piece together what *her* life was like as she approached seventy. Feeling myself drawn back to times with her, and also to times of my youth, I choose as a place for my sixty-ninth birthday getaway a place that I know will evoke those times — Newport Dunes.

It isn't until we're lined up with all the other Orange County destined "C" passengers at Southwest Airlines that Mike notices the RV designation on our resort reservation. I allow as how our reserved "cottage" is more likely to be of the pre-built type than of the quaint ivy covered white frame style he may have envisioned.

"We're staying in a trailer?" he asks, his normally sweet tenor voice approaching a not very pretty soprano range.

As with most marriages, our communication effectiveness ebbs and flows depending on our individual responsibilities, our moods and efforts, or perhaps the moon and stars. We've just come through a period of several weeks when any attempt I made to reveal to Mike my deepest thoughts were met with a blank stare, indicating that whatever was going on in his head was much more compelling to him than anything coming out of my mouth. To be fair, I know there are times when our behaviors are reversed, and I stay caught in my own head, but that story is for another time, say when rhinos fly.

Anyway, while Mike was living in his own psychic world and giving distracted uh-huhs to whatever I had to say, I arranged our Newport Dunes getaway. His getaway preference would have been the Surf-n-Sand at Laguna Beach, but at this stage of our lives it seems foolish to spend one whole month's worth of my meager teaching retirement income on two days at a posh beachfront hotel when, for a pittance, we can be in a bay-front "cottage" just a few miles up Pacific Coast Highway. Besides, it's *my* birthday treat.

The Dunes is also on the list of potential sites for my seventieth birthday celebration and this will be a good time to learn more about possible party accommodations.

I've long been leery of the temptation to spend much time in the past, fearful of reworking my personal history to fit a false pretty picture. That caution may have to do with hearing my mother's stories of her father — how jolly he was, how much fun. Her cousins, too, would say, "Oh, that Elmer. He was such a kick!" There would follow laughter over an incident during a camping trip, or a joke he'd played on someone.

When I was quite young, I yearned for the jolly grandfather I never got to meet and wished he were still alive to take me camping and include me in his jokes. Then, when I was thirteen, looking for bobby pins in my grandmother's dresser, I found a yellowed newspaper clipping that told of my jolly grandfather's suicide.

Earlier on I had noticed various adult falsehoods such as the Santa Claus and Tooth Fairy pretenses. These I'd filed in my developing brain under a category of harmless, even useful, adult fibs. My thirteen-year-old discovery of the suicide clipping, though, propelled me down the highway of cynicism and distrust from which there was no return. But now, after a lifetime of suspicion of the glories of "the good old days," as I anticipate the seventy-year mark, I find myself wanting to revisit earlier times and places, and Newport Dunes is just across the bay from a place I loved as a child.

Once settled in our "cottage," I sit in a rocking chair on the porch — a touch of quaintness that's lost on Mike as he amuses himself with the TV remote inside the spacious but pre-fab cottage.

As I look across the bay, the waning light of evening reveals a derelict piece of beachfront property that once was the site of the Bayshores Trailer Park and Campground — a place that ascends to consciousness, no matter the distance in miles and years, whenever I get a whiff of warm salt air and sandy beach. Bayshores.

In the morning I leave Mike with the newspaper and crossword puzzle and walk some distance along the edge of the bay. The sun is warm on my back — the sky a deep blue with white billowy clouds, and if I only watch the clouds, absorb the warmth of the sun, and breathe deeply of the salty, beachy air, it could be 1946. I could be eleven.

Directly across from the ghostly trailer park, I plop down at the edge of the water, in wet sand, and conjure that other time. A fence still runs along the back edge of the property, parallel to the road from Costa Mesa that ends at Coast Highway. It was along that fence, in the back row of trailers, that my granny parked her trailer every summer. Just before school was out in June, she would get someone to haul her trailer from the Garvey Trailer Park in South San Gabriel about thirty-five miles south to Bayshores. I suppose the spaces in the back row were less expensive than those closer to the beach, but it seemed a desirable location to me, where I would be lulled to sleep by muffled traffic sounds on carefree summer nights.

Off to my left, south of the old Bayshores, I scan the broad channel leading to Balboa Bay. Occasionally, when my Aunt Hazel was down for the weekend, she and I would don swim fins and tight, rubberized, Esther Williams-style bathing caps and swim from Bayshores to the Balboa Fun Zone. With money tucked high under our bathing caps we would swim past "bird island," an uninhabited piece of land about the size of a football field, where hundreds of tiny birds nested in the sand. Of course, this island now has a connecting bridge, is crowded with multi-million dollar homes, and the birds can no longer afford to nest there.

On our swim to Balboa, Hazel and I would rest at the buoys around a picturesque, old-style sailboat said to belong to Errol Flynn. We would pull ourselves up to the portholes, hoping for a glimpse of another life, but we never got much of a view.

Just past the Balboa Island Ferry dock we would swim to shore opposite the taco stand at the Balboa Fun Zone. Dripping from our swim, I would pull off my bathing cap, remove the still-dry money, and buy a dollar's worth of deep fried tacos, five, which I would eat ravenously, letting the orange grease run down my forearm and drip from my elbow. A cleansing dip in the bay was followed by several games of skee ball. It was my practice to save my skee ball tickets for one big prize at the end of summer. One year it was a silver colored statue of a dog, about three feet high, and it held a place of honor in my Temple City bedroom for many years. It was, I'm sure, the epitome of tacky, but the goals of my youth did not include acquiring good taste, and I was quite pleased with my dog statue.

Now, turning my attention away from the channel, greasy tacos and skee ball, I look across the bay to the site of the old Bayshores and draw on another memory. From fifty-nine years distance, I look backward to my eleven-year-old self as she drags the bright red, heavy wooden kayak out from under her granny's trailer and balances it on a beat-up Ryder wagon of the kind that now often graces antique store windows. She leaves the little wagon at the side of the makeshift boat ramp and pushes the kayak out a few feet, then climbs in, being careful not to let her paddle float away. Leaning against the back of the seat, she stretches her legs out straight, grasps the pole of the long paddle in both hands, and moves to deeper water on her way to Back Bay. She's not wearing a life jacket, or hat, or sunscreen, or dark glasses or amphibious shoes.

There are no buildings along either side of the bay, nor are there any boats. Except for the steady swoosh of her paddle, silence reigns. She veers toward shore for a closer look at a small, dead stingray resting peacefully at the edge of the water. Even in death, the barbed tail frightens her, and she pushes away, back out to deeper water. The muscles of her arms and back are strong and tight, and she propels the red kayak around Back Bay in a smooth, effortless rhythm.

On this conjured day, nearing the large sandbar that is a halfway mark between Bayshores and the end of Back Bay, she notices that the sun is high overhead. It is time for the eleven-year-old to return to the trailer for lunch. She is hungry, and, although her days are free and mainly unencumbered, she is expected to show up for meals, so her granny won't worry.

And now it is time for me, the sixty-nine-year-old, to extricate myself from 1946, and to show up for lunch in real time. In an effort to protect myself from more of the little skin cancers that have been cropping up over the past two decades, I take the tube of sunscreen from my pocket and reapply it to all areas of exposed skin. I roll to my side and rise slowly, from a kneeling position, with the help of my arms. Once standing, I push my right sleeve up and flex my bicep. It is still firm, though not as hard as it was in my kayaking days. I jiggle the skin on the underside of my arm and am again surprised that I've found the underside of Granny's arm attached to my own body.

Sunscreen, hat, UV protective glasses, beach shoes, loose skin and all, I take my present-day self back to the cottage. Mike sits on the porch, engrossed in the crossword puzzle. He glances up, smiling, as I flop into the chair across from him.

"What's a ten letter word for 'journey'?" he asks.

"I don't know, but I've been on one," I say.

Starts with "ex, ends in n" he says. Then, with that bolt of lightning-like word-jump he says, "Expedition! It's expedition!"

Matt and Leesa come down from L.A. to join us for the afternoon and evening. We drive to Balboa Island and, after browsing around, we ride the ferry over to Balboa. Swimming to Balboa is not a consideration.

On a balcony overlooking the bay, we drink martinis and talk of times past, present and future. The sky is still pure blue, the clouds white and billowy. Reflected light shimmers off the water. I tell of my childhood swims. The three of them look up the bay and marvel appropriately at the distance. It's impossible for them to put a twenty-three-year-old Hazel, whom they've never known as young, or an eleven-year-old me, into that picture. As connected as I am to these people at the table, I know that no one is seeing the picture I see as we gaze out over the bay.

Silently doing the math, I realize that I am now four years older than my old Granny was when I revisited her this morning. More striking still, Matt, the baby, is now older than my mother was when she and my father would make Sunday visits to us at Bayshores. And I suppose that in some future time, when I am long gone, Matt and Leesa may sit near here and bring back this martini-sipping scene, a scene others at their table won't be seeing.

Fear of the Downhill Slide
September 2005

"**J**ust take me out and shoot me," my grandmother often said after being unable to remember one or another significant detail. She knew none of us had a gun, and that if we did we wouldn't use it against her. But her wish to be relieved of a life that had become worthless to her, and burdensome to others, was quite real. I want a more workable plan than "just take me out and shoot me," and I'm hoping my offspring will help me leave this world if/when the time comes that I can't help myself. It was with this in mind that I was moved to write and send the following letter to my three grown children.

To the Fruit of My Womb on the Eve of My Seventieth Birthday:

Dear Sharon, Cindi and Matt,

Although I expect many more years of healthy, cognizant living, approaching seventy seems a good time to state in writing things we've occasionally talked about in the past. Even though Dad and I have recently made certain of our wishes known in a "Durable Power of Attorney for Health Care," the heart of such matters is mostly lost in legalese. With this letter, I hope to offer a modicum of clarity and peace of mind when you may most need it.

I remember stopping by the hospital to visit Dad's Uncle Norman one day, shortly before his death. I was shocked to see that his hands were tied to the sides of the bed to keep him from pulling at the recently added feeding tube. I asked that the tube be removed. The nurse summoned an on-duty doctor, who insisted that the removal would be a death sentence. He also was clear that there was no hope of recovery.

Although Norman was not conscious and could not express his wishes, I'd had several previous "no machines" conversations with him, and continued to ask, then demand, that the tube be removed. Finally it was, and his hands were untied.

I stayed with him a while longer, assuring him that no more tubes would be shoved down his throat. It had been days since he'd shown any awareness of things around him, and I doubt that he sensed my presence or reassurance, though who knows?

Back home, I told Dad and Matt (then fourteen) of the feeding tube incident.

"You know how he always said he never wanted to be

hooked up to any machines . . . "

They looked at me blankly.

"He was always saying that," I said.

Neither of them, though, could remember hearing Norman make any such pronouncements. Had he only told me? Did I only imagine such conversations? Was my brain playing tricks on me because I couldn't wait to get my greedy hands on his new vacuum cleaner and his Dean Witter account? I wished I'd had his "no machines" proclamations in writing.

Recently, I was with a group of contemporaries, women who were dealing with the decline of elderly parents, and I was reminded that not all decisions are as straightforward as the "no machines" decisions.

How do we find the heart and will to move those who once cared for our very own selves, 24-7, into a "facility," knowing such a move will condemn them to a sense of homelessness for the rest of their lives? Yet how can we sacrifice ourselves, spouses/partners, children, jobs, and our abundance of other modern day responsibilities, for the ongoing hopeless task of feeding, bathing, and changing our failing kin?

Woman after woman spoke of moving her mother or father out of their longtime home and into assisted care. Details varied. For some, there was a mutual recognition of the necessity for such a move. For others, there was fierce anger, with blame being piled onto the offspring, like the shovel loads of manure elders had heaved as children on farms. Sorrow and guilt lay heavy in the room.

It's been nearly six years now since I've felt the

unavoidable burden of sadness that came with every good-bye to my mother, your Granny, in her room at Scripps Home. I don't need to tell you that moving her to Scripps was the best we could do, given the range of possibilities we had to choose from. (Well . . . I guess I did need to tell you, otherwise why would I? And . . . just because I ended a sentence with a preposition doesn't mean it's time for you to put your ever-so-bright heads together and search out a "facility" for me.)

If we all get lucky, I'll simply not wake up some morning after an evening of good food, mediocre wine, and raucous laughter. But the odds are against us.

We've often talked of my desire for you to do away with me when I am no longer able to care for myself or to know what's going on around me. But here's what I know about the bunch of you. Even if I am gazing mindlessly at a spot on the wall, not knowing anything or anyone, pooping in my Depends, you may all be too wimpy to administer the overdose, or to hold the pillow over my face. If that's the case, then find a place for me, clean and well lit, as in the only Hemingway story I like. Drop by occasionally to be sure things remain clean and well lit, and to watch for new opportunities to propel me along to the other side. Please, though, take to heart that I don't want any of you martyring yourselves to the maintenance of a shell of myself. None of you has anything to feel guilty about in relation to me, and my hope is that you will never carry a burden of guilt over decisions you have to make if I someday become unable to make my own decisions.

No, I haven't been diagnosed with Alzheimer's. I haven't forgotten how to get home from Starbuck's, or left the house with the stove on. (Well, maybe once I left the house with the *stove on, but that was a **long** time ago, back when I was still cooking.) And I can still, consistently, beat the crap out of any of you brave enough to take me on in Scrabble. Boggle*, too. . . . "But at my back I always hear/Time's winged chariot hurrying near . . ."*

Now, tuck this away for a time when you may confront blank stares with the words, "You know how Mom never wanted any of us to martyr ourselves for her care and feeding . . ." Then run this missive up your flagpole, and get on with the business of living.

With love beyond words,
Your mom, who got lucky with you,
Marilyn Ann Dodson Klick Reynolds

*With the exception of iPad Boggle

Taking Care of Business
March 2008

A subject that comes up over coffee or wine, more likely wine, has to do with that nagging sense that we'd better get things in order before it's too late. Wills, finances, clearing out the attic, burial/cremation plans all clamor for our attention. I definitely want to have spelled out and paid for what's to be done with my body when I no longer inhabit it. This is one of the very rare cases in which I look to my mother as a model.

Whenever I visited Mom in her little Temple City rental, she would lead me into her bedroom, open the closet door, and point to a gray metal file box on the top shelf.

"If anything ever happens to me," she would say, "everything you need to know is in there — my burial plan, insurance papers, pink slip to the car, what I want sung at my funeral — everything." She'd started this practice sometime in her early seventies, and once started we had to go through the routine every time I visited. It was the same for my brother, Dale, when he visited.

I always got stuck on the first word of her oft-repeated speech. "If anything ever happens to me . . ." *If???* Did she think there was a possibility that nothing would ever happen to her? And then there was the next word — *anything*. I was sure she didn't mean *anything* — like winning the lottery, or being swept off her feet by some late-arriving lothario. She meant death. *If I die?* Shouldn't that be when?

Even though it was nearly seventy years ago, I can still remember the first, shocking awareness that death was my ultimate destiny. I was standing by the fish pond in Auntie Ethel and Uncle George's backyard, trying to hold still while my mother used a safety pin to reattach the sash I'd somehow torn from my dress. Holding still was not easy for me at the age of five or six, so it was lucky that I could be distracted by the statue of the naked cherub peeing his steady stream into the pond. Ever since the boy across the street from us had shown me he could pee standing up I'd wanted to know more of the mysteries of male anatomy. The peeing cherub may not have been completely anatomically correct but he held my attention.

My mother was again wishing I could be more ladylike as she tried in vain to fix the sash in a way that wouldn't show the pin. After fumbling around with it so long that even the peeing cherub had become boring, she attached the sash all cattywampus with the big, shiny safety pin in full view.

"Well, no one'll know the difference a hundred years from

now, anyway," she sighed.

"Why not?" I asked.

Usually she was loath to answer my "why" questions, but not this time. "Because we'll all be dead a hundred years from now," she said, turning away from me and walking toward the house.

"Everybody?" I asked.

She paused and turned to face me.

"Everybody who is on this earth today will be dead and gone a hundred years from now," she said. "Even you."

With that she opened the back door and went into the house, leaving me to ponder the news. Even me?

My Uncle Henry, a favorite of mine, had been killed at the bombing of Pearl Harbor and I knew I'd never get to see him again. Also, every night I prayed for the Lord to take my soul " . . . If I should die before I wake." It wasn't that I had no concept of death; I just hadn't known it was so all-encompassing.

The bluntness with which my mother was able to speak of death when she was in her thirties had, in her seventies, turned ambiguous. "When" became "if" and "death" became "anything." Yet for all of her linguistic avoidance of the inevitable, she had taken care of business and when *anything* eventually happened to her, her grey metal file relieved Dale and me of the burden of figuring out the details and making snap decisions during that emotionally charged time.

Y ears ago, when Mike and I were still almost young, I suggested that we sign up for Neptune Society services. This was after an admittedly casual conversation in which we'd both expressed a preference for cremation. He offered lip service to the idea but the day before Neptune Society "counselors" were scheduled to meet with us he called and cancelled the meeting. Since then I've probably broached the subject once every year or two, always to no avail. A few weeks ago I showed Mike a Nautilus ad.

"I'd like to get this taken care of," I told him.

"I'm not ready to go there yet."

"We don't have to go there right now. We just have to make a reservation,"

He reached for the remote and turned on the TV.

Given several decades of such conversations, I understand that Mike will likely never be ready to sign up for a pre-need cremation service. But I'm feeling a strong need to cross that item off my things-to-do-before-it's-too-late list. I expect I've got a number of good years left, but who knows? What I do know is that time passes, and so will I. In my steadfast and ongoing effort to be a better mother than my own was, I don't want to fall short at the very end by leaving all of the messy details for my kids to sort through.

After a quick Internet comparison of various funeral and cremation services, I've narrowed my choices to either the Neptune Society or the Nautilus Society. The balance tips in the direction of the Nautilus Society because their website is easier to maneuver. I decide on their "Out-of-Town" coverage, which costs only $300.00 more than their California coverage and means that, even if I die thousands of miles away from home, they will arrange for my cremation and the return of my ashes to my family with no added fee. With their local coverage, if I were to die while on a gambling spree a mere one hundred miles away in Reno, my next-of-kin would be stuck with all of the decisions and expenses required to dispose of my lifeless remains.

For several minutes I sit with my cursor poised over the "sign-up now" space next to "Out of Town" coverage. But . . . when it comes right down to it, I can't click on the button. I am, after all, in my seventies, and, although I sort of know my way around the Internet, clicking on "sign-up now" seems like a much too impersonal conclusion to my very personal end-of-life decision.

When my parents bought their "plots" at Rose Hills, first a man in a suit and tie came to our house to go over various possibilities with them. Then a few days later, on a Sunday afternoon, he picked us up in his shiny black car and drove us out to Rose Hills. I was probably about ten at that time.

What I remember about that Sunday is that the man in the suit took us to two different sections of the cemetery. The second section was somewhat more expensive than the first but, as the man pointed out to us, the view from that section was much more expansive than the view from the less costly area.

Already a realist, I remarked to my parents that they wouldn't be seeing anything when they got there, anyway. The man in the suit said the view would be for the comfort of those who were left behind.

I don't know which section they chose, but my parents bought four plots that day, one for each of them, one for me, and one for Dale. They thought it unlikely that either Dale or me would be buried there, but they could always sell the plots after we were safely grown and on our own.

I don't want to go traipsing around some cemetery with a guy in a suit and tie, or whatever the equivalent activity for a cremation decision might be. But I may actually be too old-fashioned to be satisfied with the quick click purchase. The Internet works well for books and shoes, but for arranging to have my precious body burned in a raging inferno at 1400-1600 degrees? Maybe not.

Two days after I refrained from clicking on "sign-up-now," I drive to the Nautilus address in a mixed-use area of town and knock on the door of what was once a home. A middle-aged woman greets me pleasantly and leads me to the former dining room. The interior of the ex-home is sparsely furnished, with "earth tone" walls and hardwood floors. We sit at the table, teak, I think, and she gives me the basic information I already know from my earlier Internet searches.

Although I try not to be distracted by this woman's body mass, or how far her butt hangs over the chair, or the tree-trunk size of her upper arms, I can't help wondering, will her body take a lot longer to burn than mine will?

Next I'm distracted by my conscience berating me for being judgmental and lacking in compassion. I gain control of my wandering mind just in time to answer a few questions. I'm relieved that this "pre-need consultant" is direct and to the point, not pushing to close the deal. I thank her, take her card, and leave. Back home I click the "sign up now" button, select a payment plan, review my order and click on "finish." In only minutes I receive an email back with my order number, thanking me for choosing Nautilus, telling me that my enrollment paperwork should arrive within the next five business days, and listing contact information.

When Mike brings the Nautilus Society envelope in from the mailbox a few days later he puts it on my desk without comment. It includes a basic contract and a questionnaire that asks about any non-natural devices that are implanted in my body. Apparently, cremators can be damaged by exploding pacemakers, so such devices must be removed "prior to delivering the body to the crematorium." Also the mercury in the pacemaker's batteries constitutes a significant risk of air pollution.

So far I am pacemaker free, but I promise to inform Nautilus if that changes. I sign the necessary papers and put one of the several information cards in my wallet. I'll give one to Mike, too, that he can keep on file. But I think I'll wait to do that until sometime after the martinis kick in on a Saturday night.

Tomorrow I'll go to Office Depot and buy one of those grey metal file boxes. The remaining information cards and copies of the Nautilus contract will go into a "Funeral Plan" folder, where I'll add some basic instructions for a memorial service. In other folders I'll add the pink slips to the cars, the will, mortgage information and maybe toss in a few miscellaneous items. I'll put the file on the middle shelf of my office bookcase at eye level, and at the next family dinner I'll drag the kids into my office and say, "When I die . . ."

My Body Myself
October 2007

Now that I'm high mileage, the demand for basic maintenance is taking a much bigger piece of my life pie than it once did. There's a Quick-Fit class in which, every two minutes, we alternate weight machines with aerobics machines. It's a 45-minute workout, beginning with a warm-up and ending with stretches. The workout is fine, but the music is horrendous. I may have to invest in those $200 noise-filtering headphones from Sky Mall in order to tolerate my Tuesday/Thursday Quick-Fit routines. Fitness does not come cheap.

Then there's the three-day a week Silver Stretch and Sculpt class that has nothing to do with making earrings and bracelets. It's about balance, flexibility and muscle strength — all things that wanted to turn tail and run with the extinguishing of the 70th candle. The SS&S age range is somewhere between fifty and eighty-five, but most, like me, are in their seventies. Of the twenty-five or so regulars, about half of us, the lucky ones, are working to stay strong and flexible. The other half are trying to get back to some semblance of mobility after knee surgery, or hip surgery, or having pieces of spine fused with metal screws.

In addition to the classes, I also strive to walk a bit every day. As with my writing goals — an essay a week, five pages a day on my new book — I often fall short. Ah, but I come closer than I would without a plan.

Besides the time spent stretching and sculpting, I'm visiting the dentist more often, and my doctor advises twice yearly appointments now, rather than every other year. I'm seeing the eye doctor and the dermatologist on a yearly basis. Not only that, but due to a genetic gift from my mother, I'm now on medication for hypertension. There's also a weekly anti-osteoporosis pill, and Mike's increased meds, so trips to the pharmacy are more frequent.

The hypertension diagnosis means a few minutes spent each week checking my blood pressure. Before I bought a blood pressure monitoring device, I spent days researching numerous reputedly easy-to-use, inexpensive gadgets.

None of these maintenance tasks is of an emergency nature, or overly time consuming in and of themselves, but it all adds up. Oh, yeah, I shouldn't gloss over the time spent getting reimbursement from Medicare and back-up insurance to help pay for this high-mileage maintenance.

Already I'm uncomfortable with this subject.

By the time my mother hit seventy, her conversations mainly centered on either her own medical problems, or those of family and friends, and the recent deaths of a wide range of people, some of whom I'd never even heard of until their demise. I vowed not to follow my mother's conversational lead as I aged, and here I am, stuck on self-maintenance. But the body has its claims, and it's as foolish to ignore that as it is to obsess over it.

It's not as if I've spent my life obsessing about my body! I've had plenty of other things to worry about. But I've often noticed there could be room for improvement.

(Note to body. I love you! You've kept me healthy and moving along in all stages of life. We easily learned to ride a two-wheeler. We were unbeatable at tetherball. We produced three healthy babies. Sex? Yeah. Thanks. Mostly thanks — forget Patrick Shannon Callahan. We're mobile. Steady heart beat. Strong muscles. So if I mention a few minor complaints, don't think I don't love you. Even the fat, cellulite-ridden thighs. Well . . . sort of the thighs. NO! Don't get all huffy and rebellious. I really, really, really appreciate you.)

But where was I? Room for improvement? As a child I wished to be chubby — who knows why? Probably because I wasn't. At thirteen, the only girl left in my gym class who was still wearing undershirts, I wished at least to get chubby boobs. Due to the advent of "training" bras, I suppose the loneliness of the solitary remaining undershirt wearer is no longer a threat to late blooming girls, but when I was thirteen no one seemed to know that boobs needed to be trained. At fifteen my boobs were barely noticeable; my butt, however, had embarked on the great expansion. How fair was that?

At any given time in my adult life, I've wanted to lose five to ten pounds. I still do, though the current pounds are not the same five to ten they once were. In my thirties I wanted to drop from 130 back to the 120 of my twenties. In my forties, I wanted to drop from 135 to 130. In my fifties it was 140 to 135. Sixties? 150 to 140. Seventies? 155-145. If I become one of the growing number of oldsters to reach 100 I suppose I'll forgo the birthday cake in an attempt to get back below 185 pounds.

Lately in my desire to reach the 145-pound mark, I've been considering the Mediterranean Diet. I'm fond of olive oil and hope that if I slather my whole-grained tomato-vegetable pizzas with it I'll see immediate results.

Thoughts of the Mediterranean Diet lead to remembrances of other diets — Atkins, South Beach, Weight Watchers, the Grapefruit/Spinach diet, the Pritikin diet. There was even a highly touted diet in the sixties that required drinking a half-cup of vegetable oil before each meal. That didn't last long, but maybe if it had been olive oil . . .

Recently I reminded a very long time friend that she and I once went on the Canned Peach-Cottage Cheese diet together. We were to weigh in once a week in each other's presence and if we'd lost no weight we were to pay the other person $10.00 — a significant amount for our circumstances somewhere back around 1963. Once I even tried Weight-Watchers, but it was a much too sensible plan to garner my enthusiasm.

In addition to the aforementioned myriad of diets, I've

sought a variety of other physical fixes, beginning with Vic Tanny's Pasadena gym back in 1954 and continuing up to the current Sacramento Family Fitness facility. In between, I've availed myself of the services of Slenderella, Jack LaLanne via TV, an old Canadian Air Force exercise program that required a lot of jumping jacks, a Jane Fonda audio tape, a Jack LaLanne gym (where the female instructors had bodies like Barbie and wore stiletto heels), the Pritikin Center in Santa Monica, the Pasadena Athletic Club, the Gold River Racquet Club, plus a few assorted yoga and pilates video tapes along the way.

It's true that at first glance, my long involvement with physical improvement programs may not be obvious. But, given my erratic participation, coupled with intermittent dormancy, I suppose it's no wonder I don't yet look like Michelle Obama. Well, there are other reasons, too. In spite of my 1970s Afro, I've always known I couldn't turn black. Well . . . maybe with the cremation plan, but that still won't give me muscular triceps.

The Ever Present Past
October 2006

"The past is never dead. In fact, it's not even past."
William Faulkner, *Requiem for a Nun*

At this over-seventy stage of life, layers and layers of memory lie beneath the surface of consciousness, sleeping quietly until roused by the scent of a favored aunt's Evening in Paris, or the masked hint of a song shared with one's first young love. A whiff of beer coupled with cigarette smoke and the long dead father bursts forth, pushing the present aside. The family gathers at the Thanksgiving table which is set for ten people, but another twelve or so unbidden dear and not so dear ones from the past rise up, demanding that the present be put on cruise control while they invade and dominate our perceptions.

It's not that we live in the past. We over-seventiers want to take care that the past not carry more weight than the present or future. It is a balancing act, this past/present thing, and the past is sometimes weighty and intrusive. Although the past is sometimes a nice place to visit, I wouldn't want to live there.

I did take an unplanned visit to the past a while back though, on one cold, rainy October day. It occurred to me that it was pot roast weather. It had been years since I'd cooked a pot roast. How *many* years, I wondered. A practical though unenthusiastic cook, I'd mostly stopped cooking years ago.

On a late afternoon, back in 1983 or '84, my teacher husband, having been home from school for two hours already, lounged shoeless on the couch in front of the TV and asked his usual question. He asked it before I'd unloaded notebooks and journals to be read, or taken my own shoes off. He asked it as he had evening after evening during our fifteen plus years together. Eyes still focused on the TV he asked, "What's for dinner?"

And I, for the first time in all of those years, changed the script.

"I don't know. Any ideas?"

And I sat down and took off my shoes.

As it turned out, he didn't have any ideas for dinner. So we went out that night. That night and the next night, and all of those following nights when neither of us knew what was for dinner until we read the choices on a menu.

These days, we cook at Christmas and Thanksgiving, and maybe four or five other times during the course of a year. Mostly though, we still don't know what's for dinner until we see the menu. So it should come as no surprise that when I decide to cook a pot roast I feel a need to consult a recipe for back-up. And it is only slightly more surprising to find my long dead parents hovering in the background, noticing that I'm relying on a recipe.

I suppose my mother slipped in when I reached for the cast iron Dutch oven she gave me when I set up housekeeping with my first husband, over fifty years ago. The psychic door to my father's apparition probably cracked open when I set the shrink-wrapped roast, labeled with weight and price, on the counter. What a betrayal of my heritage not to have bought from a live butcher standing on a sawdust covered wooden floor, and wearing a white, blood-stained apron. I don't exactly know what brought them forth on this occasion. It may simply have been the pot roast idea itself, conjuring up the shadowy memories of so many past pot roast dinners.

Although I'd not been the sort of daughter to take an interest in the details of cooking and cleaning, I'd been in the general vicinity of pot roast preparation most Sundays of my growing-up life. Then at the age of twenty, shortly after the wedding invitations were mailed, my mother gave me a crash course in everyday cooking, with a bit of house cleaning and laundry advice thrown in. The 1950s-mandated transition to adult womanhood offered my mother the teachable moment for which she had so long waited, and I pried open my mind to receive the handed down knowledge I'd need in order to "keep house."

As my high school sweetheart and I settled down to married life, I unquestioningly continued the Sunday pot roast tradition. Sometimes our parents joined us for Sunday dinner, or we joined them at our respective childhood homes, and the tradition flourished.

Deducting for the occasional chicken or ham, and for dinners out on Mother's Day, I figure I either witnessed or participated in pot roast preparation at least 1,500 times during the first thirty-seven years of my life — before half of my family turned vegetarian, and before I'd read *Diet for a Small Planet*. All of those pot roasts, and now I need a recipe?

I see my mother at her flour-drenched breadboard, slapping a hunk of beef around until all exposed flesh has picked up a thin layer of flour. The fire turned high under the cast iron Dutch oven her mother had given to her, she spreads a glob of lard around the hot bottom of the skillet, then adds the roast, browning it quickly. That much I remember. But do the potatoes and carrots go in now, or later? And how did she get them to be so nicely browned? I catch her expression as I glance at the recipe. It was not her way to be directly critical, but I know the look. What about a pot roast takes a recipe?

Now my father pushes forward. Seeing that the roast on the counter is a rib roast, he gives a hoot of derision.

"You may's well toss that pretty rib roast to the dog as to cook it like some 79 cent piece o' meat. Reckon all that college learnin' took away your common sense?"

"It was on special," I tell him, not bothering to update him on the general costs of meat and groceries.

"It cost less than the chuck and they didn't even have a seven bone, or a round bone."

"I don't care if they paid you to take it, you oughtn't treat it like a pot roast."

Now I'm the one traveling to another realm, transported back to our Temple City kitchen. They're in their late thirties.

I'm twelve. My father is sitting at the kitchen table smoking an Old Gold, sipping a beer. My mother is at the stove, cooking dinner. It is not Sunday, so there's no pot roast. It could be chicken fried steak. Canned string beans with a little bacon added for flavor may be simmering on the back burner. The potatoes are boiling and will ultimately be mashed. My father is talking about a customer, Miss Reed, who bought a leg of lamb but didn't have one licka' sense about how to cook it.

"'Just put it in the oven, medium heat, and cook it 'til it's done,' I told her.

"'How long?' she wanted to know. I said, 'Well . . . three pounds, probably a couple of hours.'"

"I might have said two and a half," my mother says.

"Well anyhow, she called, just before I closed. 'How can I tell it's done?'" my father says, mimicking Miss Reed's whiny voice. I know that voice because Miss Reed was my second grade teacher.

My father laughs. "'Taste it,' I said. So she asks me to hold on for a minute while she goes to taste it."

He takes a long swig of beer, savoring the moment.

"'How was it?' I asked her, when she came back to the phone.

"'Good,' she said.

"'Then it's done,' I told her. 'Time to eat.'"

With this my father's laughter erupts full force.

He gets up from the table and takes my mother's nearly empty glass to the cupboard. He downs a shot of Early Times, then sweetens her drink. He sits back down, shaking his head slowly, as if coming to a conclusion after deep consideration.

"Teachers," he says. "They know books, but they've got

no common sense. 'Taste it,' I told her, and it was like she'd never even thought of that," he laughs.

Shoving the scene from the old Temple City kitchen out of my head, I get back to my own kitchen, my own time. They're gone for a while. But I know now what I didn't know thirty-six years ago, when my father died — broken and yellowed from years of alcohol abuse. Although I wasn't crass enough to say it out loud, my secret heart was filled with relief. "Well, that's over. He's gone now," I thought. But he's never gone. Nor is my mother, either. They come back with the pot roast, or the scent of Yardley's talcum powder mixed with Early Times and cigarette smoke, or the bowl I reach for that held so many mounds of my mother's mashed potatoes. And it's not just my parents, it's the whole bunch of them — the proper ones, the drinkers, the merry ones, the kind and loving salt-of-the earth ones and the grumps.

Thanksgiving is just around the corner, and, invited or not, they'll make their way in as our children and grandchildren and all of the extended family gather around our seldom used table. In the midst of laughter and shared stories, they'll be there.

There will be Mike's Aunt Virginia, expensively dressed and doting on our son, Matt. Her husband, Norman, sitting unobtrusively in my corner. Thelma, the shirttail relative who shared our table for over thirty years, bringing zucchini bread, and humor, good will, and occasional pettiness. My grandmother, who loved practical jokes, especially those using whoopee-cushions. The believing, though back-sliding, Baptists who bring their own kind of rumbling, roiling laughter, and who used to sit around the table for hours, arguing about whether or not they'd see Mama in heaven. And even though I had given up on the idea of heaven before I reached the age of ten, even as an adult, I had felt strangely reassured by their ongoing argument.

At our real time Thanksgiving table, we will pass food for a second round, and refill wine glasses. We will talk of things past, present and future. Occasionally one of the spectral visitors will push to the foreground — remember how Aunt Gladys would get drunk in the middle of a sentence? Remember when you bet Daddy $5.00 he couldn't shimmy up to the first branch of the Sycamore tree and he marched right out and did it? And by the time he got down again, his clothes were torn and his hands and arms were all bloody! Remember those good biscuits of Aunt Willy's?

This particular year, when my eighty-five-year-old aunt leaves the table to go to the bathroom, I will be the oldest person present. The oldest *living* person present, that is. And I can't help wondering, now approaching seventy-one, what will bring me to all of those kitchens, and all of those tables where I will be showing up after the breath of life has left me. And I'm thinking maybe this is the year to remove all of my clothes sometime between dinner and dessert — so for decades to come, one or another of my descendants will say, wide-eyed, "Remember that Thanksgiving when Gramma stripped?" And I'll be welcomed as, for a moment, I come to the forefront of some future family dinner. And although I'm still not a believer, I am also still strangely comforted by the spirits of the backsliding Baptists who, if their reality trumps mine, are saving me a place at a table in their mansion in the sky.

Jack LaLanne Conjures Past Times
February 2008

$\mathbf{A}$bout fifteen minutes into my "Quick-Fit" class, I catch a glimpse of Jack LaLanne smiling at me from a TV in the far corner of the exercise room. It is an image from the early sixties, back when I was trying to get in shape after my second baby.

As Jack beams his earnest smile and buff body across the room, times past intrude on my mindless Quick Fit routine. The TV is muted and I can't read the captions from where I sit pedaling a stationery bicycle, but it doesn't matter. Like ingrained verses from a childhood nursery rhyme, Jack's words emerge from the depth of memory, urging me to take a deep breath and get into position for the "fanny firmer," or to get the circulation moving with "tummy flattening" crunches.

I am propelled back to 1960, to the Ancourt Street house in Arcadia. The baby is napping, but Sharon, nearly two, is on the living room floor with me, mimicking my exercise moves. That works pretty well until I lie on my back for "crunches" and Sharon climbs on my stomach to play horsey. Shadow, our semi-cocker mutt, also interprets floor time as play time. My exercise time is not as focused as Jack would like it to be.

Later in the afternoon, over iced tea and Winstons, my friend and neighbor, Greta, offers a critique of the morning's workout. She's irritated by Jack's dog, Happy. I, on the other hand, appreciate Happy. You never see Happy nipping playfully at Jack's Achilles tendon as he demonstrates leg lifts.

Greta also extols the virtues of Jack's "Glamour Stretcher," which she'd sent away for months ago. I can't see that her workouts with the glamour stretcher are any more effective than mine are without.

"I'll save my $1.99," I tell her.

Jolted back to the present by the demands of the Quick-Fit instructor, I leave Ancourt and 1960 to concentrate on maintaining the correct form at the "butterfly" machine. The present, though, remains compromised, and a few hours later the times conjured by Jack LaLanne push their way through again.

Facing my computer screen, seated on my ergonomically correct desk chair, I feel the cool roughness of cement block against my back and legs, as if stretched out, head to head with Greta, on the low block wall dividing our two properties, watching for Sputnik to appear, blinking far overhead across the sky. I hear her cackling laughter, her whining Scrabble complaints about never getting any vowels, her tirades over Adlai Stevenson's loss of the Democratic nomination, and her vow to be embalmed with her middle finger extended to ensure a closed casket at her funeral.

Greta's developmentally disabled son enters the scene, squatting down in the driveway beside her car, chewing and sucking on one of the tires. She rushes to attend to him.

We were young, she twenty-seven and I twenty-four, but with her severely impaired son, and her two younger sons, youthfulness was not exactly her luxury. I, on the verge of divorce, with two daughters under the age of two, was also aging quickly.

Perhaps it was in defiance of our dwindling youthfulness that, after the kids were all settled in the evenings, we ran foot races to the end of the block and back. And I suppose it was this same defiance that kept us tuning in to Jack, and exercising every weekday morning, Monday through Friday.

What I wanted back in the old days with Jack LaLanne was to get in shape for summer so I would look good in a swimsuit. I wanted to wear my red sheath dress without having it pull too tightly across my baby-wide butt. These days, at Family Fitness, my thoughts are not on either a bathing suit or a sheath dress. The bathing suit would expose too much of my already compromised skin to cancerous sunrays. Even worse, the sheath dress would expose my grandmother's gently undulating folds of skin hanging loosely from the backsides of my upper arms. No, my present goals do not involve anything remotely resembling either a bathing suit or a sheath dress. They have to do with maintaining a modicum of strength and flexibility, and fighting the inevitably losing battle against the ravages of time.

My visit to 1960 was brief. Though other layers of memory have clamored for attention — the neighborhood Fourth of July celebration, the heated presidential election, my young brother Dale's presence in nearly every scene — they must, for now, be sent back where they came from. This beautiful day, with petals of pear blossoms lightly falling like snowflakes outside my office window, is not to be ignored. Nor is the dog, poking me with her cold wet nose, reminding me it is time for a walk. We will walk.

First though, in spite of having long ago realized the futility of questioning the randomness of life and death, I pause to wonder why it is that I will walk, breathing in the sweetness of approaching spring, and Greta will not? Why is it that I have been given the luxury of reaching a healthy old age and she had less than sixty years of life? Futile, unanswerable questions.

I'm grateful I still walk this earth and sorry Greta doesn't. Grateful also that her laugh still lurks beneath the surface, waiting to spew forth with the image of Jack LaLanne, or a rack of Scrabble letters heavy with consonants. Grateful that tomorrow's workout will be in the aerobics room, where there are no TV screens to conjure up who knows what remnants of the past. As long as no one standing next to me smells of my father's cigarette smoke and stale beer, I may get through the next workout in the present tense.

Senior Moments
Anytime

Remember when a "senior moment" had to do with the prom or ditch day? Around 1996 that phrase shifted meaning to describe times when we oldsters suffer a momentary lapse in memory. We search for the word that was there when we started the sentence, but has fled the scene by the time we try to complete it.

"Oops. Senior moment," we say.

Or we see our neighbor at the market, not a close friend but someone we've known for years, and we can't remember her name. We walk into a room and stop, not knowing what we wanted to do there. Frustrating and perhaps worrisome.

We know that some memory loss is part of the aging process and we figure we're okay as long as the senior moments aren't interfering with our daily lives. We make lists. We write notes to ourselves. We keep our calendars handy. We pay attention to articles that shed light on how to maintain or improve our memories. If we believe in a God who listens we pray that our lapses in memory don't portend the onslaught of Alzheimer's. If we're not believers we simply hope to escape the Alzheimer's epidemic predicted to blossom within the next few years.

There is a great fringe benefit that comes with momentary memory loss, though. The book about those three old lady characters that we read a long time ago? You know — they were constantly drinking beer. They lived in a place surrounded by a wall made of beer bottles? Oh, damn! What was that book??? And then, a few minutes, or hours, or days later, the title bursts forth, like a gift from heaven. *Suds in Your Eye, Suds in Your Eye*!!

Whatever frustration accompanies a lost memory is miniscule when compared to the nearly orgasmic pleasure that comes with retrieval. It's better than the prom or ditch day ever was. Bring on the senior moments. I'm after cheap thrills.

Stuck in the 20th Century
Now

To say that many aspects of the tools of modern technology baffle me is an understatement. Although I've come across a few middle-old tech whizzes, most of my over-seventy peers share my state of tech-bafflement. We still think tweets and twitters are what the birdies in the trees do.

Who knew that the grandbabies we taught to patty-cake and to ride those little horsies up to town would soon be programming our cell phones for us, sometimes in ways we don't want and don't know how to change. I'm sorry if the other grandkids are offended because sixteen-year-old Subei's picture fills my cell phone screen whenever I turn it on, but I don't know how to change it back to its previous generic image, much less how to add a more equitable group picture. Here's what I can do with my cell phone. Make phone calls.

Answer incoming phone calls. I've always thought that was what phones were for.

Here's what I *can't* do with my cell phone. Get directions when I'm lost. Amuse myself with a game of Scrabble. Surf the Internet. Check my email. The grandkids can do all of those things on my phone but I'm still back in the 20th century, using my phone for phone calls. Oh, and I forgot about texting. That's another thing I can't do with my phone. I suspect those in the under forty range communicate more by text messages than by conversation. I can't get the hang of it. When someone texts LOL, do they mean little old lady, or laugh out loud, or lots of luck, or lay off legumes? This whole texting craze seems like a process ripe for miscommunication.

One day last week another middle-old friend and I had lunch with a middle-middle. He was ecstatic over his new iPhone and eager to show it off to us. We were dutifully impressed but neither of us thought we'd add iPhones to our accumulation of misunderstood tech-devices.

What was most impressive about our friend's new phone was that *his* state of the art cell phone will talk to him! It has the voice of a woman and her app is SIRI. (I just recently learned that "app" is short for application, and it has nothing to do with moisturizer.)

Want to know the location of Istanbul? Ask Siri and she'll tell you within seconds. The population of Egypt? She's got it. The major points of FDR's New Deal? That, too.

Our friend amuses himself by asking Siri such questions as "What is the meaning of life?" The interesting thing is that she offers a variety of answers including, "I don't know, but

I think there's an app for that," "I find it odd that you would ask this of an inanimate object," and, my personal favorite, "All evidence to date suggests it's chocolate." At first I found it strange that her answers to this one question were so varied — maybe it was a programming error. Then I considered how inconsistent my own assessment of the meaning of life is and decided that she varies her answers for the sake of seeming more human.

Sometimes our friend asks Siri sexually provocative questions. Unlike simple questions like the location of Istanbul or the population of Egypt, he didn't ask such questions in our presence. Perhaps he thought we were too old for that kind of talk. But he did tell us that Siri usually answers such questions with "Don't be naughty."

I know they're miracles, these cell phones with Internet access, GPS, and speech capacity, but lately I find myself wondering, as my old Aunt Ruth did when they finally got electricity in her Arkansas town, "What *is* this world coming to?" If I had an iPhone I'd ask Siri.

To See Ourselves
as Others See Us?
Maybe Not a Good Idea
January 2011

$\mathbf{R}$obert Burns, the 18th Century Scottish poet, is likely most famous for a few lines lifted from "To a Louse," a poem of eight stanzas generally neglected except for:

> "...*O wad some Power the giftie gie us*
> *To see oursels as ithers see us . . . "*

Translated to modern English as "Oh would some power the gift give us, To see ourselves as others see us."

Bobby Burns wisdom aside, it may not be an advantage to us seventy-plussers to see ourselves as others see us. Such a vision brings the awareness that a less vital, competent and attractive version of our true selves is floating around in the atmosphere, distorting perceptions of friends, family, and strangers alike.

So it is sometimes shocking to have reflected back to us a less competent and attractive vision of ourselves — like the vision that came to me at the local Super Cuts.

I try to change my hairstyle every decade or so, and recently realized that it was probably a year or so past time to leave the very short, spiky style behind and find something different but equally easy to maintain. Short of shaving my head it was hard to imagine what that style might be. Then I came across a picture on a promotional flyer that showed me with short hair, but full, a sort of wedge in the back as I remember, though that view was not shown in the picture. I recalled liking that style. I think it was easy.

The flyer had been unearthed from a bulging old file box I was bent on emptying.

As the author of a series of ten teen fiction books, I'm sometimes invited to visit high schools and talk with students about my stories, the writing and publication process, and whatever else comes up.

I was fifty-four when my first book, *Telling*, was published. At times when I see advertising material for the series I'm momentarily taken aback — almost as surprised as any of my old high school teachers would be to know that I'm a well-published writer, so I probably hold on to writing related memorabilia longer than is truly reasonable or necessary. Hence the rediscovered flyer for a visit to Pasadena High School.

The picture on the flyer was taken from the back of *Too Soon for Jeff*, the book listed as my most recent. Jeff is the story of a reluctant teen dad, published in 1994. So, okay, the picture was about seventeen years old. It was done professionally and perhaps a few wrinkles had been airbrushed out, but still . . .

I take the picture to Super Cuts and show it to Kwan, my regular hair-cutter.

"Can we work toward this style?" I ask.

She studies the picture.

"What do you think?"

"Sure," she says. "Let top and sides grow to same length — keep back short."

Handing the picture back to me, Kwan says, "Your hair more wavy. Won't look exactly like hers."

Hers?? *Hers*?? She hasn't even recognized me. I'm sure I've changed a little over the past seventeen years, but am I presently unrecognizable from my 1994 image?

"Keep hair picture for next time," Kwan advises.

I tuck the flyer back into the inside compartment of my purse without revealing to Kwan the true identity of the woman in the photo. Watching in the mirror as Kwan cuts my hair, I don't think I look all that different from '94. But since I'm not wearing my glasses my face is a blur.

Back home I stand before the bathroom mirror, glasses on, and take a good look. I see this same face in this same mirror every morning — rubbing in lotion, applying lipstick, darkening my graying eyebrows, applying a touch of mascara to my thinning eyelashes. But my morning routine has me only looking at separate parts of my face at a time, seldom standing back for a look at the whole. As I do so now, I see that Kwan must be forgiven for her failure to see me in the picture.

A few weeks ago Betty, who is in her mid-eighties, told me that she no longer looks at herself in mirrors. "I feel the same inside as I've felt my whole adult life. I don't like seeing the outer changes."

I wondered how she managed her morning tasks without looking. I guess one really doesn't need a mirror for applying lotion, or brushing teeth.

"I stopped using any sort of make-up when I turned eighty," she said. "A waste of time and money and I don't have enough of either left to spare."

"What about your hair?"

"Clean and brushed," she said.

Her hair, short, white, full, looks at least as good as mine, better on most days. Maybe I should follow her example — save time and money, and not open myself to Bobby Burns' sought after gift. Or I may wait until I'm eighty, like Betty did. Only four years to go, the fact of which is a much greater surprise than actually seeing my whole face in the mirror was.

The Big Questions
My So-Called Spiritual Journey
Background, 1938-1943

W ith longevity's gift of perspective, and leisure time for reflection, I sometimes find myself contemplating long held beliefs, and disbeliefs — revisiting experiences that built the foundation for what might loosely be described as my philosophy of life.

B ecause of my early Sunday School experiences, Jesus played a significant part in my own youthful search for answers to questions of creation and eternity. The very first dream I can remember was from a time when I was probably four years old, or less, because I hadn't yet learned to swing by pumping my legs. In the dream I am small and lonely, sitting in one of four swings in a playground. I'm gripping the chains that attach to the sturdy supporting metal frame. The seats are made of a rubber-like material that curves upward at each side of my light body. There is sand underneath my dangling feet. The children in the other three swings each have a grown-up standing behind them, pushing, laughing, offering encouraging words.

I sit in my becalmed swing, watching the others riding up and down, up and down, and I'm fervently wishing for someone to come push me. Just give me one little push! I'm only wishing, not even praying, when a man comes walking toward me. He is surrounded by a soft, glowing light and he's wearing a long white dress. He smiles at me and I smile back. I think he is Jesus, the one from the Sunday School picture who talks sort of funny, saying stuff like "Suffer the little children to come unto me."

I feel safe. I already like Jesus because of that song about how he loves me, and also because he's a friend of my Granny's.

He doesn't speak. He just walks around behind me and gives me a push. His hands against my back are so gentle I hardly feel them, but the push is so strong it sends me soaring. I fly higher than I've ever been, back and forth, back and forth, never losing height or momentum. It's thrilling but not scary and I know it can go on and on and on.

I don't remember how the dream ended. Maybe it just drifted away with the rhythmic movement of the swing. What I do remember is that the very next Sunday I'd rushed into my classroom to look carefully at the picture of Jesus. He was definitely the one who had given me a push. That Sunday I sang "Jesus Loves Me" with great fervor and enthusiasm.

The first hairline crack in the foundation of my faith came when I was probably around six. The boy across the street told me there was no such thing as Santa Claus and only babies believed there was. My mother assured me there was definitely a Santa Claus and I couldn't trust everything Richard Metz said. But I'd been put on alert and it took no time at all to realize that the Santa stories were lies and that Richard Metz was more trustworthy than my own mother.

Once I'd learned the truth about Santa, I developed nagging doubts about God and Jesus, who both fell into the same too-good-to-be-true category as the magical man with the flying reindeer. But the adults around me seemed to take God and Jesus a little more seriously than they did Santa, and I wanted to believe, so I continued to say my prayers and to think God might be listening.

The next fissure in my faith foundation came when I was around eight years old and Granny took me to Angelus Temple, the church of the famed Aimee Semple McPherson.

I often spent Saturday night with my grandmother in her trailer down on Garvey Boulevard in South San Gabriel. Sunday mornings we would ride a city bus to the corner of Hollywood and Vine. From there we would walk a few blocks to The Little Country Church of Hollywood where we would hear the Goose Creek Quartet sing about Jesus, and Sister Sarah would read letters that testified to the joys of salvation after lives of horrible sins. The preacher's name was Fagan (I don't think I'm making this up) and he delivered his Bible wielding, fire and brimstone sermons with great passion. I was captivated by the watery spray that punctuated his pleas for surrender and his promises of salvation. Decades later, when a professor of linguistics referred to "plosive consonants," Dr. Fagan's spray leapt to memory.

Although Dr. Fagan sometimes spoke for so long that my butt hurt, I sat quietly without squirming because if I was a good girl, and I always was, Granny would take me to the Pig-n-Whistle for lunch. The menus there doubled as masks of cute pig faces and I could always make Granny laugh by donning the mask and oinking. It was many years before I recognized the irony of the adorable pig faces on one side of the menu and the link sausages on the other.

Why Granny had chosen Angelus Temple rather than The Little Country Church of Hollywood on that particular day is now lost to me. It may have been that some well-known missionary was speaking. If I've got the timing right the year was 1943. Sister Aimee was probably there in her flowing white gown but as memorable as she was reputed to be, I have no memory of her that day. What I do remember is the spectacular testimony of the featured missionary's salvation.

He began by speaking of his mission's work with heathen sun god worshipers in darkest Africa. There was a wobbly movie of near naked black men dancing in a jungle clearing in frantic homage to the brightly shining sun. Then the same men were shown clothed and subdued in prayer before a large, white cross in a wood frame church.

Here's the part that really got me, though. In a dramatic accounting, punctuated by light and sound effects, the missionary told of how he had been a terrible sinner, living in thrall to the devil, speeding toward an eternity in the fires of hell. God kept calling to him but he wouldn't listen. He was an atheist!

As the missionary spoke of a night when God had been particularly insistent, he walked from the podium to center stage and entered a previously unlit set — a replica of the kitchen where he had once lived. On the table was an ashtray overflowing with spent cigarette butts, opened and apparently empty cans of pork and beans, and a nearly empty bottle of whiskey. The convincingly realistic sink and counter along the back wall of the set were filled with dirty dishes.

In sharp contrast to the Godless filth of the kitchen were the pretty gingham curtains that decorated the window above the sink — the only remaining evidence of the loving wife who'd been driven away by her husband's sinful ways.

Leaning against the table in the midst of his own squalor, the missionary told of his decision to put an absolute end to whatever crazy notion of God had been hounding him. Gathering himself to his full height he gave the air above him a violent punch upward as he cried out, "God, if there be a God, let him show Himself unto me!" He stood for a moment in the silence. Then, both fists lifted toward the heaven he denied, his voice amplified by unseen microphones, he cried out again, "God, if there be a God, let him show Himself unto me!" Again . . . silence.

At his third, ear-shattering demand, "God, if there be a God, let him show Himself unto me!" a sustained roar of thunder rocked the very space around us. A blindingly bright ball of light shot through the window, shattering the glass and surrounding the doubting sinner as he dropped to his knees in terror. The voice of God, deep and resonant, answered.

"Here am I. Walk in my light!"

Although the cliché had not yet entered our daily speech, it is safe to say of the missionary's experience, "The rest is history."

At home the next evening I could barely wait for my mother to leave to pick my father up at his market. I'd been waiting all day for the time I'd have the house to myself.

"Don't you want to go with me to get Daddy?" she asked.

I shook my head no, not meeting her eyes. Usually I'd have gone with her. I liked to be in the market after closing time, to help scrape the blocks clean and get a quick snack of sliced cheese or a bite of raw hamburger. But I had more important things on my mind right then.

"Well . . . I won't be long," she said. "If anyone rings the doorbell, don't answer it."

As soon as I heard the car leave the driveway I went to the kitchen and raised my fists heavenward. I hoped my mother wouldn't be angry about the shattered window.

"God, if there be a God, let him show Himself unto me!" I called out with all my might.

Brownie came running in from his warm spot by the fireplace in the living room and stood in front of me, ears perked forward in a way that implied a question.

I stretched even taller, took a deep breath, waved my fists even more forcefully and shouted, "God, if there be a God, let him show Himself unto me!"

Brownie barked and jumped at me, wagging his tail, then crouching in his "let's play" posture.

For my third plea to God I stood on the kitchen chair, reached even closer to the ceiling and bellowed out, "God, if there be a God, let him show Himself unto me!"

Brownie's barks matched the volume of my pleas and we went on like this, Brownie barking and me shouting to God until the headlights of the Pontiac flashed across the window. I jumped down from the chair and slid it back where it belonged. By the time my parents walked through the door, Brownie and I were stretched out in front of the fireplace in a tranquil domestic scene, me with a book propped on my chest and Brownie with his nose resting against my leg.

I pretended to be engrossed in the book, but really I was contemplating the lack of evidence for God in my life. If God had come to the sinning missionary but not to me, what good was He anyway?

The seeds of cynicism grew and, although I continued to attend church with my grandmother and sometimes Sunday School at a church near my home, I couldn't give my heart totally to God as I was supposed to do because He had not appeared to me that Monday evening when I tried with such eager anticipation to summon Him.

Now though, having revisited that long ago time of my life, I wonder, did I miss something that evening? I cried out to God and Brownie came running, and with each shouted plea, Brownie tried harder and harder to gain my attention. And I'm thinking, maybe my young mind didn't totally understand the GOD/DOG/GOD reality, and God really had come to me, standing before me, wagging His tail and barking His head off.

Just a Thought —
More of How Others See Us
Or . . . Fantasies
of a Misunderstood Oldster
May 2009

Within moments of arriving at the bleacher-less soccer field where my granddaughter is playing, two people stand and offer me their portable chairs. I am of an age now. Assumptions are made.

At a Thai restaurant the handsome Asian waiter assures me that the dish I've ordered is "not too spicy."

"Then can you make it more spicy, please?"

"No problem," he says, jotting something on his note pad.

Still, when the dish arrives it is bland, as if he, with his elegant high cheekbones and caramel colored skin knows better than I what pleases my taste buds. But I don't send my food back to be spiced up. The assumption that I prefer bland food is bad enough. Worse would be the assumption that I'm a cantankerous old crone.

When the waiter returns halfway through our meal to ask if everything is okay, he gives me a slightly patronizing smile — the kind I'm too frequently seeing these days. *I make eye contact and hold his gaze until he looks away. Wondering what he tastes like, I stand and lick his handsome face. "Ummmm, spicy," I say, as he turns his head to offer the other cheek . . .*

Just a thought.

With only the briefest glance toward a Nordstrom's cosmetic counter, an eager sales clerk presents an outrageously expensive wrinkle-defying potion for my perusal. The smooth-skinned young beauty advisor, eyelids not yet drooping, throat skin taut, does not place before me the new summer line of hot-pink colors—no glossy, luscious, strikingly bright, sexy, kissable lips for me. My main task is to defy wrinkles.

"You'll see a noticeable difference from the first application," she promises.

The noticeable difference I would see would be in my checking account balance, a figure that's frightening enough as it is. But I wonder, does this enthusiastic youngster believe the claims of the wrinkle-defying product?

"You're sure?" I ask. "A noticeable difference with the first application?"

"Absolutely," she says, oozing sincerity.

"I'll take it!"

"You won't be sorry," she says.

Once the purchase is completed, I remove the miracle product from the tasteful Nordstrom's bag.

"I don't need this," I tell my advisor, handing back the bag.

Opening the chic little jar and turning to face the mirror on the counter, I rub a generous amount of the substance into the left side of my face. I go over that side one more time, careful to leave no patch of skin untreated.

I hold the mirror closer to my face.

"Amazing!" I say, angling the mirror slightly to the left, then right, then back to the left again.

"You're right!" I tell my beauty advisor. The volume of my voice and the intensity of my pleasure is now attracting attention.

"Look how much smoother the left side of my face is!"

My advisor offers a nervous smile and a slight nod of the head.

I turn to a nearby customer.

"Look! Just one application! See the difference? You should try it!" I call after the woman who is now rushing toward the escalator.

"I owe it all to you!" I say, turning back toward my advisor whose hand now hovers inches from the telephone receiver.

"Thank you so much! I can't wait for my husband to see the new me!" I say, slathering the cream on the other side of my face.

"Just evening things up."

I take one last adoring look in the mirror. "I truly can't thank you enough," I gush. My advisor picks up the receiver and touches the keypad as I walk through the exit to the parking lot . . .

Just a thought.

At an upscale steak house (also not good news for my checking account balance) I order a T-bone steak, rare.

The waitress smiles down at me with her glossy, luscious, strikingly bright pink lips.

"That would be quite bloody in the middle," she says.

Stretching my lightly tinted, wrinkled, beige-rose lips to return her smile I say, "Please. Quite bloody in the middle."

"We just like to be sure," she says.

A few minutes later, when the young man at the table next to ours orders his steak rare, I can't help noticing that our waitress doesn't seem to feel the same need to be sure with him. Nonetheless, I, who have never had to wait tables except in my own dining room and even then don't do a very good job of it, forgive her assumption that I'm more of a well done than rare person. And the steak does arrive quite bloody in the middle. Tender, juicy, cooked to perfection. So what if my beige lipstick will be completely worn off by the time I take the last bloody bite?

Tucking the napkin into my blouse, bib style, and grabbing the steak with both hands, I pull off chunks of bloody flesh, using my canines the way they were meant to be used. Pinkish dribbles of grease slide unwiped from my mouth to my chin. I gnaw my way closer and closer to the bone, emitting low growls as I devour the most succulent meat of all. I rid the bone of all traces of meat and marrow and finally, satisfied, I sit back and express my pleasure with a magnificent burp . . .

Just a thought.

It's a Big World After All
2006 or Anytime

For a week or two, back when I was twelve years old, my desire for a grown-up job was to be sent to Africa as a missionary where I would spread the gospel and save heathen souls. However, after a bit of my own soul searching I realized that I myself was more heathen than Christian and bringing souls to Christ would not be a good career match. Still, a residue of missionary spirit remained.

In the late sixties and early seventies I was actively involved with a church-related group that emphasized works more than faith and, with other congregants, I expressed my latent missionary spirit working to ensure that the Fair Housing Act was upheld in our little southern California town of Temple City, a town that once required home buyers to sign an agreement stating that they would not sell to anyone of African, Asian, or Latin descent. I marched against the war in Vietnam, led study groups on that subject, and helped convince local churches to stop paying their telephone tax. That was my life related to the big world. In my small world I was devoted to my two, then three young children, my new husband, our extended families, and my newly embarked upon teaching career.

In 1972, after a brief hiatus from teaching to be with my youngest child during his pre-daycare days, I took a position as an English teacher at an alternative school in southern California. For the sake of brevity let's just call the alternative high school A.H.S.

As with so many mothers of young children I took the job not because it was ideal but because it offered a work schedule that was most compatible with my after-school mom responsibilities.

It didn't take long to discover that nearly all of the A.H.S. students came from low income, often troubled families, and that their previous school records were dismal. Most of our students had been kicked out of their home high schools and this was their last chance at graduation.

The focus of my missionary efforts soon shifted from global issues of peace and justice to matters directly related to A.H.S. and its students. I still tried to be informed on national and world events but, except for having strong opinions, I was not involved beyond the close boundaries of our family, and the school and the district in which I taught. Although I sometimes berated myself for not being actively involved in causes I so strongly believed in, I took comfort in knowing that my occasional success with getting a student connected to reading made a significant difference in that student's life.

Each year at A.H.S. there was a core group of students who worked hard to make up credits and earn their diplomas. About half of our 180 or so students, however, stayed for only a few weeks to three or four months, and then they were gone. Some went to stay with a relative in another town, some got sent to juvenile hall, or they were pregnant, or had work hours that were incompatible with school, and on and on.

I myself had been a poor student in high school. I didn't do homework and I didn't read assigned materials and I barely squeaked by. But I read. During English classes, behind the thick anthology, Frank Yerby or Mickey Spillane books often lurked. *Forever Amber, The Caine Mutiny,* and any other number of popular books of the day had their turn at hiding behind various textbooks.

Nine years after high school I decided to go to college. I hadn't been a good student since the sixth grade and wasn't sure I could function academically in college courses. But I could. Between high school and my entry into college I'd read, among many other titles, *Dr. Zhivago, Fountainhead, East of Eden* and nearly everything else by John Steinbeck, *Peyton Place, Lolita, Advise and Consent, The Robe, Exodus, Hawaii, The Egg and I, Kon Tiki, The Blue Book of the John Birch Society*, and parts of the Bible. As a budding English major I sometimes wished my reading tastes had been a bit more highbrow. I wasn't one of those students who could toss around titles of books and names of authors that would impress professors. But I was, in my own way, an accomplished reader. And through extensive reading, as if by osmosis, I'd absorbed good writing skills.

I knew the power of reading books of one's own choosing and I turned my missionary tendencies to the task of getting every student who walked through my classroom door hooked on reading. If they took with them a reading habit when they walked through that door for the last time, they would have a chance to gain perspective on whatever lay directly ahead of them. At the very least they would have a healthier means of escape and entertainment than was often available to them.

Of course a few A.H.S. students already knew the joy of reading, but most did not. Once I could find a subject or author that interested a student we were on our way. *The Outsiders* and other S. E. Hinton books were popular. *Are You There God It's Me Margaret* was a hit with the girls. Stephen King worked for some of the better readers. Mostly what my students wanted, though, were books that reflected something of life as they knew it, and at the time there weren't nearly enough of such books around.

After years of frustration at finding so few books my students could relate to, I decided to try writing one. The first novel, *Telling*, was the story of a girl who was being molested by a neighbor. It was a hit with my mostly reluctant readers. The next was a teen pregnancy story, *Detour for Emmy*, also a hit with my students and with a broad range of other readers. Halfway into my next book, a teen pregnancy novel told from the boy's viewpoint, I opted for an early retirement to free up writing time. Prior to that, my writing had been at night, on weekends and holidays, and during summers. I was eager to get back to a reasonable work schedule. My retirement agreement included twenty-five days of work for the district each year for five years — a perfect balance.

Since retiring I've had published eight more books of realistic teen fiction and a book for teachers, *I Won't Read and You Can't Make Me: Reaching Reluctant Teen Readers*. Each of the teen fiction books takes on a difficult situation that teens are sometimes faced with, situations of the kind many of my students had faced. Molestation, pregnancy, rape, gender identity — tough stories but all ultimately portraying the strength of the human spirit.

Early on in my retirement, still with that skewed missionary spirit, I sometimes felt guilty for no longer personally engaging in the tough and sometimes rewarding task of teaching the mostly disenfranchised. Then I would get a letter from a reader on the other side of the country, telling me that one of my books had made a difference in his/her life, and I would be reassured that my books were doing good work out in the world. Although the vast majority of responses to books in my Hamilton High series are positive, accusations that I am a pornographer, or that I'm leading the youth of the nation astray, occasionally show up in my email, or in my old-fashioned mailbox.

Back in 2005 enough people concurred with these accusations that one of the teen pregnancy books, *Detour for Emmy*, was included in the American Library Association's Top Ten Banned Books. That definitely enlarged the dimensions of my broader world. When I heard the news that *Emmy* was on the list, I whooped for joy. There it was, on a list that included books by J. D. Salinger, and Judy Blume, and Mark Twain. We were in great company!

I rushed upstairs to share the news with Mike, then sent

the equivalent of a cackling email to friends and family. Mike opened a better bottle of wine than our usual Two Buck Chuck, and we toasted my newfound fame.

I envisioned my book featured prominently in displays in libraries and book stores across the nation during September's "Banned Books Week."

If every bookstore in all fifty states bought just one copy for display, would I finally be able to upgrade my aged Volvo?

I visited the American Library Association's Banned Books website and saw the 2004 banned books bracelet that featured the covers of the top six books for that year. Cool! My book was number six. If ALA kept the bracelet idea I could walk around with *Emmy* on my wrist and show off to cashiers at the supermarket, and to manicurists at the mall.

In spite of my advanced years, wisdom is not always the controlling factor in my first response to whatever comes along, so it was not until I awakened with my customary three a.m. ruminations that my better self pushed to the surface, dog paddling frantically through waves of pride, and greed, straining for a glimpse of the bigger picture.

In the early morning darkness, curled close against Mike, lulled by the soft, steady snore of Sunny the Schnauzer on the chaise, I thought about the total list. What's the deal with the morality police, anyway? At a time when we're bombarded daily with reports of violence in the schools and on the streets, they've only attacked one book for violence, and that book is *Captain Underpants*??

The other nine books, *Emmy* included, made the list because of sexual content and/or offensive language. American children are sixteen times more likely than children in other industrialized nations to be murdered with a gun, and the book banners' greatest fears are for sex and bad words? And back to *Captain Underpants*, which, in addition to violence, made the list for anti-family content and for being unsuited to the age group. Excuse me? Bathroom humor not appropriate for five to twelve-year-olds? All I need say to get my five-year-old granddaughter laughing uncontrollably is "poopie." For the eleven-year-old, "flatulence" works well.

Then there's Chris Crutcher's *Whale Talk*, which, besides being dinged for offensive language, was cited for racism. Really, although *Whale Talk* does confront issues of racism, the book itself is about as racist as the writings of Nelson Mandela.

The more I thought about it, the angrier I got. Where do these limited, small-minded, ignorant, people get off, trying to keep books out of the hands of readers?

Afraid that the intensity of my anger might somehow be transmitted, body to body, I moved away from my peacefully sleeping husband. Then my ruminations took a turn. Why am I the one awakened every morning around three by the spirit of Mimi, the Grand Goddess of the Harmonic Universe (see "My So-Called Spiritual Journey, Part II," page 103), demanding that I consider carefully all disharmony in my life and in the world? Why can't I be like Mike, or the dog, and sleep soundly through the whole night?

I glanced at the clock. It was 3:43. In the past twelve hours I'd committed four of the seven deadly sins: pride, greed, anger and envy. Could I get to the remaining three before daylight?

With a bit more prodding from my better self, I realized

that I'd fallen into the same trap as the would-be censors. In questioning how they could ban so much sex and so little violence, I was putting my values above theirs. I could write a lengthy treatise on why my values are better for the world and everyone in it, but that's not the point. Noam Chomsky said it best when he said, "If we don't believe in freedom of expression for people we despise, we don't believe in it at all." It turns out, I do believe in freedom of expression, and that includes the expression of those who would ban books in general, and mine in particular.

Sin or not, I am proud of *Detour for Emmy*. I think about the letters I receive from readers, letters indicating that Emmy's story offers insight and perspective on their own lives.

" . . . I just wanted to let you know that your books have led me into the world of reading. I started with *Detour for Emmy*, and now I've read all of your books."

" . . . This book encourages me to not get pregnant at a young age because when I pretend I'm Emmy I realize . . . she had to change her plan and goals of life. I wouldn't want that to happen to me . . ."

" . . . your book has inspired me to keep my legs closed."

" . . . I'm a sixteen-year-old mother and Emmy's story helped me realize I can make a good life for me and my baby. Thank you."

My heartfelt wish is that every censorship attempt would backfire in the same way a Texas grandmother's push to ban *Detour for Emmy* from her local schools did. Several months after that unsuccessful book challenge, the librarian wrote:

You would not believe how many of my girls at school have

*requested the opportunity to read your book. I have several paperback copies from the **Emmy** challenge, and I just hand them to the girls and ask them to return them as soon as they are finished. They always bring them back and tell me how much they enjoyed the book and how much they learned. That challenge may be one of the best things that happened to the girls at my school!*

As the first rays of light crept in through cracks in the blinds, I decided to finish off the seven deadly sins. Rubbing sleep from my eyes, I planned a day of lust, and gluttony, and sloth.

My daytime hope, before the three a.m. Grand Goddess could get to me, was that the morality cops would launch a nationwide campaign to ban *Love Rules*. It's a wonderful story, with sex between two girls and a smattering of offensive language, and is deserving of attention.

At this over-seventy stage of life, I count myself lucky to still have a small presence in this big world.

Reinvention Ruminations
Spring 2011

Mike now resides in a memory care facility where he receives the close attention and monitoring that is necessary for his own safety, and for the safety of others. The move, just after Christmas of last year, was one of the most heart -wrenching experiences of my life. But, as promised in the preface, those stories are for the next book. This is about reinvention — the other side of heart-wrenching.

If not for the unfailing emotional and practical assistance of friends and family during these recent tough times I would, by now, be as dotty as a dodo. This core group of supporters has earned the dubious honor of membership in the 100-Hours Club. One hundred hours is probably a gross underestimate for the times these people have lent their helping hands and listening ears, but one of the gifts of longevity is a relaxation of standards of mathematical accuracy. Besides, these are not the sort of people who keep track of their good deeds.

It was with the help of the 100-Hours Club that, within days of Mike's move, I rented a P.O. box and stored everything but a few clothes, my laptop, a plastic file of important papers, and Sunny's dog bed, and left the retirement community where we had been living.

For most of my life, changes of address were few and far between. The time at Carmichael Oaks always felt tentative and temporary, but that was exceptional. I was thirty-seven before I ever lived more than eight miles from the house I grew up in. Then there were twenty-five years in Altadena, all in the same house, and then twelve years in Gold River. Staying put was what I liked best, and then suddenly I was a nomad, carrying with me from place to place a carload of basic necessities.

I'd come unmoored, uncertain where and how to drop my anchor. I knew it would be in the Sacramento area, not far from Mike and close to the 100-Hours Club members, but how to make it happen? The idea of living alone for the first time in my life didn't frighten me, it was simply beyond the realm of my experience, as was renting a house, or an apartment.

I housesat for three different sets of friends who were vacationing at conveniently staggered times, and who were not averse to having Sunny in their homes. Between house sitting stints I stayed with Dale and Marg in Sacramento, Sharon and her family in Woodacre, Matt and his family in Walla Walla, Washington, and I also visited friends and family in southern California.

Halfway through the Walla Walla stay my sixteen-year-old

granddaughter, Subei, flew up to join us, and to ride back with me on my return. She was a great traveling companion and it was not lost on me that I'd luckily caught her just before that time when the adults in her family would suddenly turn stupid.

Although I was experiencing a disconcerting sense of being unmoored, I was also enjoying my newfound freedom. Not since being a teenager under my parents' roof had I had so few daily responsibilities. If I wanted to read all night and long into the morning, I could. Sunny would keep me from sleeping beyond eight or so in the morning, but once her minimal needs were met I could sleep the rest of the day if I felt like it. I never felt like it, but the *possibility* was thrilling.

Unlike a house-sitter we once used who let slip information she could only have known through reading a personal letter that was tucked into a back corner of my bottom desk drawer, I was careful to respect the privacy of the people who had so generously let me stay in their homes. No foraging through drawers or medicine cabinets, no messing around with papers in files. Do unto others, etc. But I couldn't help noticing various kitchen set-ups. The set of dishes, bowls and cups stacked neatly in a deep drawer next to the sink. What a good idea! So much more convenient than having to reach for them in a higher cupboard. And the top-of-the-line cookie sheet in another house. It was so solid, and easy to clean! I vowed never again to buy a cheap cookie sheet.

I'd always disparaged the cone and cup process of making coffee, but that was all that was available in one of the houses. After a few weeks of using that formerly disrespected system

I was converted. Then there were the towels. Unlike the basic binary toilet paper decision of over or under, it seemed there were countless varieties of ways to fold towels.

In years past, Mike had been the one who folded our towels and he'd used the tri-fold method that doesn't show any edges. One of the houses I stayed in had the towels folded in half, lengthwise, and then in thirds. Another house folded towels in half, lengthwise, and then doubled over. One rolled the towels tightly and stored them on an open shelf where they added color to the otherwise muted tones of the bathroom. I wondered what procedure I would follow when the day came for me to be folding, or rolling, my own towels.

Besides picking up hints for orderly living while house sitting, the relaxed and unencumbered times between houses, staying in the homes of the people I most love, was a luxury I'd not experienced during the past few years. I'm aware of Benjamin Franklin's wisdom about how fish and houseguests smell after three days. I hope no one got the scent of fish before I packed up and went to the next place. My visits were admittedly longer than three days, but I was unobtrusive and low-maintenance and their doors are so far still open to me.

Hmmm . . . "Unobtrusive and low-maintenance." It strikes me that my mother-in-law might have said the same thing about her stays with us, and I distinctly remember getting a whiff of fish just moments after she'd unpacked her bags.

A recent cartoon in the "New Yorker" had a past-their-prime couple sitting at a table across from one another. The wife is saying to her husband, "When one of us dies I'm going to live in Paris for a year." She was, I would guess, anticipating her reinvention. I, too, was anticipating my reinvention, though Paris didn't figure into my plans.

My personal re-creation mainly focused on the place I would soon settle into. As generous as the 100-Hours Club had been in offering me a variety of ports in the storm, I'm pretty sure they would tire of me if I continued my nomadic rotations indefinitely. Besides, I longed to have my own space, sleep in my own bed, sit on my own couch, eat from my own plates.

I began surfing the net for possible rentals. I noticed "For Rent" signs as I drove from place to place trying to get an idea of what might work for me. Occasionally I made an appointment to look at a duplex or apartment. I quickly learned the language of rental ads. "Cute Cottage" equals dump. The same with "Quaint." "Cozy" means it's a ten by ten box. "Classically Remodeled" — a hodgepodge. No price listed in the ad — overpriced. "Friendly and Attentive Landlady" — chatterbox with no boundaries.

Mike's monthly out-of-pocket memory care bill is hefty, so a downtown loft with a view of the capitol was out of the question, as was the newly refurbished house just down the street from Dale and Marg's. But in spite of budget restrictions, I had a list of requirements that I hoped to hold to. I wanted two bedrooms, one of which could be my office. Having lived in a house with four bedrooms for the previous twelve years, should two bedrooms be too much to ask for?

I wanted central heat and air. It gets very hot in Sacramento in the summer time, and colder in the winter, too, than my native southern California. Even after twelve years, my body remains acclimated to the weather conditions of my native environment. Below seventy degrees and I'm wearing gloves and fleece jackets. Above eighty-five? Give me the artificial breezes of cool air.

The convenience of a dog door is something both Sunny and I enjoyed for many years. Okay. Two bedrooms, a dog door, central heat and air. Also, I wanted a garage, preferably attached so that on rainy days I could go directly to my car without getting wet.

The place wouldn't need a bathtub. A simple shower would do. I could do without a dishwasher, but not a washer and dryer. Oh, and storage — at least two very large walk-in closets with abundant cabinet space in the kitchen, like the Gold River house.

I wanted room for a table that could seat at least six comfortably. I'm not through having friends in for dinner. A patio with enough yard space for Sunny to run around in. I wanted flowers and trees, maintenance included. Oh yeah, and a quiet location — quiet but still walking distance to stores and a light-rail stop and a Starbuck's. It didn't *have* to be a Starbuck's, just a Starbuck's-*like* place. There should be a library and bookstore nearby. I wanted a view of the river.

No need for hardwood floors, good carpeting would be okay. Light. It would need plenty of light. And a landlord who provides meticulous maintenance, not just of the yard but of everything else, also.

I was eager to get my things out of storage and have them at my fingertips. One of the things I missed most in my vagabond life was my clothes. Of course I have some clothes with me — I'm not running around naked. But that pretty green silk scarf — is it in a box along with so many other boxes in the Harveys' barn? In a drawer at Sharon and Doug's? In the chest of drawers which is tightly bound with something akin to shrink-wrap, covered with a large, quilted pad, and securely positioned in the impossible-to-get-to back corner of the storage unit? And what about my bathing suit? My new place should have a swimming pool so I'd better find that bathing suit.

I think my accent color will be red. In the past I preferred subdued colors but the reinvented me will be bold. I won't paint a whole wall red, but maybe the woodwork, or the doors on the many kitchen cabinets. (Note to self: Add permissive to landlord qualification.) A red lamp in the living room would pull things together nicely. Maybe I'll get one of those adult sized tricycles, red, with a big enough basket that I can carry groceries in it. Maybe I can train Sunny to sit in the basket.

Why was I only thinking about a place to live? So much more of my life needs to be reinvented. All that Mike and I were together as a couple is gone. I have to reinvent my life as a woman living solo. Not exactly single, but solo nonetheless.

It would be a mark of my reinvention if I did something I've never done before. I don't mean like shopping at Nordstrom's instead of Macy's. Something big, like running a marathon, or climbing Half-Dome, or cooking something from *Gourmet Magazine*. Oh, oops! I forgot. *Gourmet Magazine* is no longer being published. Okay. Maybe taking up Sudoku puzzles or dog sledding the Iditarod trail. Something. Plus working on the next book — *Approaching Eighty and I Don't Mean Miles Per Hour*. Or I could take up throwing horseshoes competitively. It's brave new world.

I can't wait to get back to things I've loved but not had time for. These past few years the only time I could read for any extended period was sometime between one and three in the morning when I would awaken with worry. Then I'd reach for my teeny-tiny book light, my glasses and my book, and read for an hour or two. But now, daytime reading! And exercise. Finally I'll have time to perfect my body.

Reinvention — The Reality
December 2011

So, no, I couldn't find the place of my dreams that would fit my limited budget. But I came close enough. It's still more than I *should* be paying, but the Goddess Mimi and I had a long talk while I was on the lookout for a place to rent. We decided that I'm too old for delayed gratification, and that the quality of my life counts for something. So I made a year's commitment to a place closer to my fantasy.

I moved into the chosen apartment in mid-July, again with the help of the 100-Hours Club. Having helped me with three moves within these past fifteen months, I'm guessing they're all happy to know I've signed a lease and they've got at least a year's respite from the moving business.

The apartment has a surprising number of characteristics included in my fantasy checklist. Two bedrooms, so I have a separate office space. I am delighted to have my printer, office supplies, files containing business papers, tax information, contacts with teachers and librarians, and personal journals chronicling decades and decades of my life all back within my reach. The constantly moving, nomadic persona faded quickly, replaced by the steady, grounded persona that is so familiar and comfortable to me, and that has served me well throughout my life.

So yes, the fantasy criteria of two bedrooms was met. *Maybe* I can squeeze six people around a table in the dining area, though it would help if two of them were under the age of ten. Central heat and air — check. No attached garage, but a designated covered parking space a short distance from the apartment. Storage space is a far cry from my fantasy, though there's a walk-in closet in the master bedroom and a reasonably large closet in the "office."

The kitchen is tiny with very little cupboard or counter space and a less-than-desirable electric stove. I'm not too worried about the kitchen though, because I hardly ever cook anyway. You're wondering about those six-people dinner parties? Within a one-mile radius of where I now live there are at least ten good restaurants that can provide tasty take out meals. Some even deliver.

My walking distance to stores and Starbuck's fantasy? Got it. No view of the river but just a short walk to the levee. The grounds are pretty, though there's no yard for Sunny to run around in. There is a nice pool and a small gym, and although it's near two busy cross streets it's amazingly quiet.

The manager tells me the residents are about half retirees and half college students. So far there's been no raucous noise though I suppose that could happen some weekend night. You know how those retirees are.

The hoped-for washer/dryer was not to be. That's the greatest minus in a sea of plusses. There's a laundry room with coin-operated washers and driers just across the pool from me. The machines are in good condition. The room is clean and never crowded. It's open 24/7. So it's mostly a matter of organizing things differently than I'm used to. It is not a great hardship, but I'd be playing the Pollyanna Glad Game in the extreme if I said the laundry arrangements were all fine by me.

I find that I'm accumulating larger loads before I make use of the laundry room. And the old style of sorting with whites, light/medium colors, and dark, all in separate loads? Gone. Now I jam everything together, drop in my six quarters, and hit start.

There are a few delicates that I don't want to submit to my new laundry practices so I'm washing them by hand. The problem with that is the burden of environmental guilt that goes with my hand-washing process. Two or three years ago guilt caused me to break my longtime habit of brushing my teeth in my morning shower. For the sake of water conservation I shifted my brushing locale to the bathroom sink, using the least amount of water possible to get the job done. It was the right thing to do.

Maybe that shift occurred after seeing the Al Gore documentary, "An Inconvenient Truth." That was probably about the same time we shifted to those silly looking, environmentally friendly light bulbs.

Since I gave up brushing my teeth in the shower, switched

to the funny lightbulbs, and became a recycling fanatic, my conscience has been fairly clear in terms of how I'm treating the environment. But now I am again struggling with environmental guilt, and again it has to do with water use. No longer brushing my teeth in my morning shower, I'm now doing half of my washing there. Don't scoff if you haven't tried it. It's very convenient and I'm loath to change my ways, though my conscience may again get the best of me.

At seventy-six I'm living alone, on my own, for the first time ever. I was the one in charge (sort of) for several years when Sharon and Cindi were little and before Mike and I got together, but that was a very different household than the one I'm in now. As far as the living space goes, I'm mostly reinvented. When it came right down to it, I wasn't quite brave enough to paint anything red but my toenails. The apartment could use a few decorating touches, a dash of color here and there, but I'm waiting for my style to evolve.

For over forty years, Mike and I were in a near-constant state of compromise when it came to home decor. My bent was to keep things sparse and simple and I probably wanted that more in the extreme as a reaction to Mike's tendency to fill every shelf, table, wall and corner with *things!* He prided himself on his good taste but, really, there was too much of it.

How will I choose to put things together when not reacting to Mike's decorating tendencies? I know the Hummels and the ornate vases and the little candy dishes won't be sitting around. The overdone silver tea service complete with the showy silver tray will remain carefully stored until hell freezes over, or until someone I care about wants it. So I know what I won't do. But what *will* I do?

So far I'm keeping things minimal. The two pieces of lightweight sculpture decorated with designs found on Anasazi pottery shards are on the wall as they had been in Gold River. It was such a rare occurrence for us both to fall in love with the same piece of art that we bought the first one on the spot. The other sculpture was a combined gift from our family for our twenty-fifth wedding anniversary.

I'm very fond of both of those pieces and expect to have them on display for the duration. The "Spider Woman" Navajo rug that Mike always insisted be displayed hanging from the wall is now on the floor. It's a *rug* for goodness sake!

I wonder if over time I will latch on to something else — catch some collecting bug? African masks? Sculptures of nudes? WWII posters? Will I develop a particular style? I doubt it. I think non-style may be my true style. We'll see.

The less tangible part of my reinvention is a work barely in progress. Who will I be as an ostensibly single woman? Will I call couple friends and suggest a movie, or meeting for dinner? Will they call me for the same purpose? Or will I, more likely, call another woman, either one who does things on her own without her husband, or one who is also single?

Mike is the one who got tickets for the symphony, or concerts at the Mondavi. I doubt I'll be doing that. Will I miss it? Something else that remains in the "to be seen" category.

Although the evolution of my social life and my sense of style is not yet determined, other aspects of my reinvention are quite clear to me. From writing for a teen audience to writing with my contemporaries in mind is on its way to becoming a reality.

The idea of developing and marketing writing classes for the over seventy population is still just that. An idea. But my experiences leading a writing group at Carmichael Oaks tell me there is a great need for such classes, and the leadership task is rewarding.

Although I'm shifting my writing focus to a much older audience, I still like visiting high schools. As long as teens remain interested in my books, and interested in meeting me, I'll keep saying yes to those invitations.

The plan to perfect my body? Well . . . each day I walk Sunny at a leisurely pace four or five times a day. If I'm particularly energetic our total distance for any one day may reach two to three miles. Three mornings a week I've been walking/jogging on the treadmill at our little gym, something to get my heart rate up, though the truth is I only jog for thirty seconds every five minutes so that hardly counts as "interval training."

At each of the positions on the Universal-like apparatus I lower and lift the weights ten times. That's ten times on a very light setting. All upper body "work." So the perfect body may yet elude me. I'm probably not even doing enough to count for the "vigorous" exercise that so many new studies are showing to be important in maintaining cognitive function.

Okay, excuse me. I just reread the previous sentence and it scared me.

Now I'm back from a vigorous walk, followed by leg lifts, bicep curls, and tricep extensions, all executed holding matching heavy cans of chunky applesauce.

A lot of over-seventiers are working on their travel

"bucket" lists. For me, for now, most travel is out of reach because of budget constrictions. But earlier on Mike and I did a fair amount of travel together, so I'm not feeling travel-deprived. And I'm grateful we had those experiences while Mike could enjoy them.

Probably the most ambitious travel on my immediate horizon will be more road trips to Walla Walla. That's manageable. My Walla Walla grandaughter is five and I want to be as regular a part of her life as I can. I'm not nearly as sought after by the older grandkids as I was when they were five and I want to take advantage of my status with Mika as a sought after companion while it lasts. Of course I want to see her parents more often also. I know they love me and they always welcome me, but they may not be as out-and-out thrilled with me as Mika is.

A few days with the Reynolds-Kyle bunch is always fun. Their downstairs apartment makes for a great writing retreat, though I don't have much need to retreat from anything in my newly invented life.

I know that the heart-rending sadness of Mike's condition and decline will always lie heavy in the Mike compartment of my heart. I know that other less wonderful reinventions will ultimately need to be made. If I'm lucky I'll deal with some of those experiences in *Over Eighty and I Don't Mean Miles Per Hour.* For now, though, Ethel Merman is strutting across the synapses of my mind belting out "Everything's Comin' Up Roses," though really, it's petunias.*

*See My Favorite Flower," page 89.

Grandparents' Day
November 2011

It is Grandparents'/Special Friends' Day at Marin Academy, the Wednesday before Thanksgiving. Subei, my sixteen-year-old granddaughter, meets me at the sign-in desk, schedule in hand, and together we go to her first two classes of the day, Spanish 3 (honors) and Astrophysics, both classes conducted in languages I don't understand.

Subei and I get our picture taken together after Astrophysics, then go our separate ways, she to another class and I to the reception where I sip coffee, nibble coffee cake, and observe the crowd of grandparents gathered in the too small space.

From what I hope is a discreet distance I watch as a man who looks to be in his eighties holds a tiny taste of coffee cake to the lips of his wheelchair-bound, palsied wife. She sits slumped over, head down practically to her lap. A stroke,

I suppose, or some other devastating turn of events. He is gentle with her, and patient, and I wonder about their earlier lives, raising the mother or father of the grandchild they're visiting with today. I wonder about their empty nest years. Had they renewed the earlier spark, which had been dulled by the worry and work of those childrearing years? Sometimes that happens.

I watch as he carefully maneuvers the wheelchair through the crowded room, getting a head start on the next event. I hope they got one of those empty-nest renewals. I hope it was a renewal strong enough to keep him up to the task at hand.

For the last event of the day the school's four hundred students, faculty and invited guests gather in the gym. I find a seat on one of the lower bleachers, next to another middle-old grandmother. As we wait for things to get started we exchange stories, as grandparents often do, of our grandkid's talents and escapades. With just the slightest tinge of envy, we compare what we've seen here today with our own 1950s high school experiences.

In keeping with the spirit of Thanksgiving, students express their heartfelt appreciation for selected M.A. teachers and other staff members. They offer examples of the help, humor, support, and guidance that "their" person has provided for them. Those singled out for such praise don't know ahead of time that they're being honored, and as they come forward to receive their book, or flowers, or some other memento, the ease and affection between staff and students is a joy to witness.

The very strong emphasis on academics at M.A. is

equaled by the emphasis on the arts and creativity. Except for the scattered and impressive expressions of gratitude, the hour-long program consists of music performed by various combinations of students. From duets to groups of ten or so, the pieces feature a variety of instruments including acoustic guitar, steel guitar, drums, keyboard, violins, bass, cello, accordion, flute, and banjo. Several of the singers also play instruments.

One young woman solo-whistles a whole chorus of one of the songs. Her whistle is strong and tuneful, and it gets me thinking about how unusual it is these days to hear anyone whistle a tune, and what a common sound that was during my growing up years.

I take a short visit to 1941, to the just-built house next door to where my parents and I live and where I listen, fascinated, as our new neighbor, Dorothy Horton, whistles a magnificent rendition of Chattanooga Choo-Choo while lining her kitchen cabinet shelves with flowered paper. Dorothy Horton. At least ninety if she's even alive. Still young in my memory.

Today's music is a good mix for this audience of mostly older folk. There is a Beatles' song, and something from Joni Mitchell, there's an ensemble piece — part tango, part classical, and something by contemporary composer Leonard Cohen. There are also a number of original works written by M.A. students. All are performed with grace and precision.

During one of the longer lulls, as the members of the ensemble are setting up, my bleacher-mate tells me that she has more energy now than she's ever had. But it's just the

opposite with her husband. He'd always been very athletic
— full of energy for hiking, swimming, running marathons,
you name it. They'd often taken challenging hikes and all-day
bike rides together. Now all he wants to do is sit around. "It's
hard for me," she says. "But I finally decided that just because
he sits around all day doesn't mean I have to. There are plenty
of other hiking and biking opportunities out there. Things
change," she says, smiling. "I'm readjusting my life."

I think of the couple that had earlier caught my attention.
Such a readjustment for them. And I think of Subei, so bright
and lively reaching toward the fullness of adulthood, also a
time of readjustment, of reinvention. And as the next set of
musicians present a familiar Joni Mitchell song, the lyrics
seem universally appropriate:

And the seasons they go 'round and 'round
And the painted ponies go up and down
We're captive on the carousel of time
We can't return we can only look behind
From where we came
And go round and round and round
In the circle game.

Reinvention Reality
My Favorite Flower
Late Summer 2011

Some months back, the writing prompt for the Carmichael Oaks writers' "homework" was to write about their favorite flower.

I don't want to set myself up as some sort of expert who is above doing the same things I ask of those in the group, so it was with some consternation that I sat down to do my "homework" on an evening in April. As is often the case once I get situated to write, I'm struck by what a mundane, superficial prompt I've suggested. My favorite flower? It sounds like a subject my third grade teacher might have come up with. But fair is fair.

I first thought of roses, the long ago spicy scent of a particular bright pink rose my mother often brought in from the garden.

Then the daylilies planted from bulbs brought back from our cousin Neva's yard in Arkansas. My first orchid corsage. The profusion of camellias nearly every place I've lived. (Disclaimer: The referenced replanted bulbs and profusion of camellias were not under my care. I simply enjoyed them.) The pleasing, potent fragrance of a gardenia. Hydrangeas, with large, intense blue flowers of the sort that grew in my grandmother's yard. All of these flowers I love. But if forced to pick a favorite the everyday petunia always wins hands down.

Whatever the opposite color of green is on the color wheel, that's the color of my thumb. I've stood by and watched many plants die — fuchsias, gardenias, Corsican Mint, hydrangeas, chrysanthemums, daisies, you name it, they've all come to my place to die. I don't really get it. I'm literate. I'm conscientious. I know how to read and follow instructions.

Somehow, though, the moment a plant sees me reach for it at the local nursery the die is cast, and I do mean die. Within a week of being carefully planted exactly according to instructions, the plant will have committed suicide in some secret way that I cannot counteract. They all hate me. They would rather die than live in my presence. Except, that is, for the ordinary petunia.

Petunias love me. They sense we have a lot in common. We're not remarkable for our beauty, though we often add a touch of color to the scene. We're not prone to disease and we're not finicky. We're hearty. We have an affinity for one another.

The day I moved into my new, not exactly fantasy style

apartment, Dale suggested we make a trip to the nursery and find some things with which to brighten my approximately 8' x 10' patio. There is a concrete slab with a strip of bare dirt, about two feet wide, running the length of it. Except for the sliding glass doors that lead out to the patio from the living room, it is surrounded by a drab-brown, five-foot-tall solid wood fence. Brightening the patio seemed like a good idea.

Dale and I share some genetic tendencies — absent-mindedness, a taste for martinis, a love of low stakes poker, but whereas plants self-destruct when they see me coming, Dale need only look at raw dirt for something either beautiful or tasty to sprout. He is referred to by some as Mr. Green Jeans. So Mr. Green Jeans took me to Green Acres Nursery where we proceeded to pick out hanging baskets and plants to go in them. Dale pointed to a beautiful fuchsia plant loaded with delicate pink and purple flowers.

"No way. I'm already into the triple digits with the number of fuchsia plants that have died in my presence."

"It would be just right! It likes shade. It cascades. We want things to cascade from the hanging baskets."

"Nope. Let's get some petunias."

"Petunias?" he asks, incredulous. "Petunias need lots of sun. Except for a very short time in the late afternoon, your patio is all shade."

"I don't kill petunias," I say.

"Maybe not, but they'll die of their own accord without sun."

We choose an asparagus fern, a sweet potato plant with very dark red leaves, and something with small white flowers that I can't name, but is pretty and will, I'm told, cascade.

"Look at those cascading petunias," I tell Dale.

He laughs. "Do you notice they're in the sun and not under the shade canopy?"

"I think they like me."

He laughs harder.

Will, the owner of the nursery, stops to talk. Because Dale is such a frequent customer, it seems he's on a first name basis with every nursery owner/worker in the area. He introduces me to Will, then tells him of my desire to put petunias in a shady area.

"They'll die," Will says, and leads us to other cascading shade plants while he and Dale talk their gardening talk.

We choose a tuberous begonia. I don't think I've ever had a tuberous begonia so there's no history of sudden plant death attached to that choice.

We have one more hanging pot to fill. I go back to the petunia section.

"I'll try this one," I say, adding it to the cart.

"I hate to sell you a plant that I know is going to die on you," Will says.

"I promise not to hold it against you," I tell him.

Dale allows as how there *might* be enough sun at the very corner of the patio to keep a petunia alive for a few days.

Plants for all five hanging baskets accounted for, we go over to the pottery section where I choose six 5" pots, all with a deep red glaze. These will fit nicely on the board that tops the fence. Again we choose those little white flowered plants that love the shade, and some with little blue flowers. Having given up trying to talk sense to me, Dale stands stoically by as I select petunias for two of the pots.

After adding little Corsican Mint plants for ground cover, and potting soil and soil booster to the cart, we check out to the tune of $172.69 and head back to the drab patio.

I'll admit that Dale did nearly all the work — filling the baskets with soil and booster, adding the chosen plants, hanging the baskets, then taking on the smaller pots. I occasionally handed him something, stood back and admired his work and maybe brought him a glass of iced tea. I don't really remember the iced tea part, but I hope it's true. The last task was preparing the strip of soil not covered by cement, then planting the ground cover starters. Maybe I put two of those plants in the soil. I probably did because they died within days.

Before sunset the patio was bright and cheerful — a huge improvement. Oh yes, and the wind chimes were hung, too. A few days later, we made another trip to Green Acres, this time with Sharon. She bought an Abutilon plant, with dark red flowers guaranteed to attract hummingbirds. "We" planted it at the corner of the fence where it can be seen from the living room. It was, she said, a housewarming gift.

Since the Abutilon is not yet in full bloom I added a hummingbird feeder, and some familiar decorative items that were saved from our Gold River patios. The patio is now a very inviting space for a cup of coffee and the newspaper in the morning or maybe a glass of wine and pita chips in the evening.

Now, after two months or so, everything is doing well except the plants with the little white flowers, and the plants with the little blue flowers. Even though I took care of them according to instructions, they all died. Maybe it's because I never learned their names. Ah, but the petunias? Blooming! Thriving! Cascading! All of them, the ones in the little pots and the ones in the hanging pots. White, purple, pink, they keep blooming, not requiring much, happy to add splashes of color without showing off. They're role models for my reinvented life. If I were younger I'd have another daughter and I'd name her Petunia.

The Gifts of Longevity
December 2011

What a friend we have in time
Gives us children, makes us wine
Tells us what to take or leave behind.

"Friends With You," John Denver

This time of year elicits a multitude of scenes of Christmases past. I know there've been varying degrees of imperfections in every holiday season and, if pressed, I could dredge up an unhappy incident or two, or twenty. But like Melville's Bartleby the Scrivener, I prefer not to. One of the great gifts of time is, in the words of John Denver, that it "tells us what to take or leave behind."

I take with me the children of Christmas, my own and others in the family, and then the grandchildren, and those who first showed me the joys of Christmas, my grandmother, parents, aunts and uncles. Like turning the page in a Pop-Up book, parties and crowds of friends and relatives make their surprise appearances, then fold back into the past, making way for the present, some of which will find its way into next year's Pop-Up scene.

The sip of eggnog, a scent of pine, the dog's new squeaky toy, a long familiar carol, span the decades of scenes worth keeping. With the first taste of a sugared walnut, my friend Greta from our Jack LaLanne days pops up. Her laugh. Her outrageous take on life. Her good heart. The gifts denied her with the denial of longevity.

Her life was not easy — whose is, when it comes right down to it? But her difficulties were balanced with humor and love and joy. What a gift it would have been for her to have more time with her treasured granddaughter, to travel with her, live through the teenage years with her, enjoy her early entry into adulthood. On the other hand, things could have turned sour. Best not to mess with the gifts that might-have-been — best to stick with the gifts that are.

What a bonus to have grown-up friendships with my adult kids. And to witness, and sometimes participate in, the trajectory of their own kids' lives from babyhood on. And friends from as long ago as elementary school. Really, there's nothing quite like being reminded in the company of other less well known acquaintances that in the sixth grade you tackled and pummeled the school bully. At least it was the bully and not someone smaller than I was. And who else is there who remembers and is impressed by my award for being the wittiest girl in my tenth grade class? The friend who was honored with the male equivalent of the same award. That's who.

Then there are the less easily described gifts that go with longevity. I've grown comfortable with just being me — comfortable in my own skin, to use today's vernacular. I'm not saying I can no longer be sorry for some thoughtless remark, or embarrassed by an unplanned fart. I don't especially *like* to fart in company but, as with most middle-oldsters, farts happen. So??? If anyone thinks *that*'s worth a second thought then they don't have enough to think about.

Forgiveness is another of those precious intangible gifts. For decades I kept remnants of anger tucked away in a tiny treasure chest and buried in the dark side of my heart. I sometimes liked to lift the lid on the chest and revisit anger. There was anger at my father for drinking himself into an early grave. Anger at my mother for her boozy, whiny neediness. Anger at my first husband for doing me wrong. Then one day when I went to visit my treasure, the anger was gone. I looked in the corners of the chest. I even ripped out the lining, but it was nowhere to be found.

I dragged the chest out into the light to get a better look. It had to be there somewhere. But it wasn't. Besides that, not only was the anger gone, but it had been replaced by gratitude. When I was a child my father read to me, and joked around with me. He taught me that being honest, holding fast to one's good name, was all-important. Gratitude for his gifts to me overcame anger at his weakness.

My mother took good care of my physical needs and I grew up healthy. She also offered a powerful example of what practices and attitudes to avoid in my own mothering style.

No small gift.

As for my first husband, it's true he did me wrong, but no other DNA combination would have produced the two unique and irreplaceable daughters that we got started together. For that I am ever grateful.

Maybe the best part of the gift of forgiveness is that I forgive myself for the uncountable big and small mistakes I've made. That's not to say I'm happy with them all, but I know that I, like most everyone else, have done, and am doing, the best I know to do.

The years have taught me to accept reality. Even though I'm not a believer, I've said the Serenity Prayer often enough that sometime over the past few decades it sank in. As an agnostic I drop the God part of the prayer and skip right to "Grant me the serenity . . ." I hope that deletion saves me from hypocrisy. The idea of working to change what I *can* change and accepting the things I *can't* change is so common that it seems trite. I don't care. It keeps me from spending precious energy tearing my hair out over the unchangeables — my hair that is unchangeably less than thick and luxurious, but is acceptable.

I suppose the more up-to-date equivalent of accepting the things we cannot change is "It is what it is." Oops! This simple supposition has led to an extreme case of dilly-dallying and shilly-shallying that has sucked the time out of my morning.

First, I decided to see if "It is what it is" is in fact more up to date than the serenity prayer. This led me to a 2004 article from *U.S.A. Today* referring to the phrase as a *sports* cliché, and quoting numerous coaches and athletes as proof. I don't watch sports. The sports section of the newspaper is recycled without a glance along with the ads, and the topic of sports comes up in conversation with my friends just a little less often than string theory. I was certain "It is what it is" reached far beyond sports talk. I searched for evidence to support my opinion.

When I admitted how incompetent I am with modern technology, did I mention the Google exception? I *can* Google. In fact, one thing often leads to another and I Google all day and far into the night. There are times when I behave like those rats that are given two buttons to push, one that releases food and one that activates the "pleasure center" in their brains. Given the choice, the rats frantically and repeatedly choose to press the pleasure stimulation lever over the lever that releases food and water, ultimately dying of dehydration and exhaustion.

So far I always take a break from Googling for food and drink, but it was before breakfast this morning when I started the "It is what it is" searches and I'm on the verge of Googling straight through lunch.

Anyway (Have you noticed that people under the age of fifty say "anyways?" What's *that* about?) Anyway, the amateur Internet word buffs claimed a wide variety of origins. One said the phrase was first used in 1999 by some football coach. First used in 1999? I don't think so. Another referred to a letter sent by a hermit, Noah John Rondeau, to the editor of an Adirondack Mountain newspaper back in the early 1930s. He ended his letter with *"It is what it is."* So HA! to the *stupid* idea that 1999 was the first use of the phrase.

Even so, in one form or another the serenity prayer has been around much longer. Clear back in 1695 Mother Goose

said: "For every ailment under the sun/There is a remedy, or
there is none;/ If there be one, try to find it;/If there be none,
never mind it."

The first written record of today's version of the serenity
prayer was in a widely circulated sermon by American
theologian Karl Reinhold Niebuhr (1892-1971). Shortly after
the publication of that sermon, Alcoholics Anonymous began
using the prayer in Twelve-step programs in the early 40s,
and, as they say, the rest is history . . . Hmmm. When did *that*
phrase became so popular?

If we count the Mother Goose rendition, certainly in
keeping with the sense of things, my earlier supposition that
the serenity prayer has been around much longer than "It is
what it is" holds true. But if we require that the wording of the
prayer be a more exact match to today's version, it's a close
call. So I'm going with Mother Goose.

Now that that mystery has been put to rest, shall I close
Google for a lunch break? Apparently not, because there is
dilly-dallying and shilly-shallying.

I know what it means: to occupy one's self with trifles
— describing what I am doing so well at this very moment.
I'm thinking I heard the phrase from some vice-presidential
guy. I doubt it would have been Gerald Ford — too many
syllables. I think the phrase is too silly to have escaped Hubert
Humphries' lips. Lyndon Johnson? I try to translate dilly-
dallying and shilly-shallying into Johnson's Texas dialect. It
seems impossible that he *could* have pronounced the phrase
without speech therapy. Just to be sure though, I Google
Lyndon B. Johnson quotations.

No citing for d-d and s-s, but I found something that puts

him in the "it is what it is" camp. He said, "Being president is like being a jackass in a hailstorm. There's nothing to do but to stand there and take it."

Spiro Agnew! Why didn't I think of him in the first place? I Google Spiro Agnew quotations with almost as much zeal as the rats pushing their pleasure center button! It's got to be old Spiro! I know he came up with some doozies, like "Once you've seen one slum you've seen them all." As with the other Googled vice presidents, I draw a d-d and s-s blank with Mr. Agnew's quotes, too. I am, though, rewarded with a laugh over the reminder of "nattering nabobs of negativism."

Suddenly I get one of those gifts from the universe. The dilly-dallying and shilly-shallying speaker *was* a vice-president, only not a U.S. vice-president. About thirty-five years ago he was the V-P of our local teachers' organization!

Anyway. Anyways. This is quick: "anyways," according to a writing tips blog, is: "a colloquial corruption of 'anyway.' . . . It might help to remember that 'anyway' is an adverb, and adverbs can't be plural."

Why didn't I think of that?

You're wondering what any of this has to do with the gifts of longevity aren't you? I'll tell you. Time to shilly-shally and dilly-dally is a great gift. Time to follow one's own impulses, to let curiosity be the guide, to take a whole hour, or a day, or a week to do what one wants. I *love* this part of being a middle-oldster.

Sunny lies half-asleep, bored, on the chaise near my computer. She needs a walk. So do I. But now I'm wondering where "*Que sera, sera*" fits in the "Grant me the courage to change that which I can . . ." and "It is what it is" timeline?

And was that Doris Day? Or Dinah Shore? And are they still alive? And what about "doozie? And that's the way the cookie crumbles"? The answers to those and so many other questions are floating around in cyber space, just waiting to be Googled.

I'm afraid the rest is history.

My So-Called Spiritual Journey
Part II
1992 to Now

I never experienced the sought after bolt-of-lightning message from God that would eliminate all doubts, though I later had something akin to a religious experience.

Did I make this up? I don't know. It seems as if it happened.

It is the Christmas season, 1992. Hollywood Presbyterian Church. I am sandwiched between my eighty-one-year-old mother, Esther, and her seventy-year-old sister, Hazel, in a pew near the front of the Hollywood church where my husband is the tenor soloist. This is a place my mother and aunt love and I can barely tolerate.

The last time I was here, over a year ago, I went in feeling fine and returned home with such a severely stiff neck that I couldn't turn my head more than half an inch in either direction. It was an extremely painful condition and it lasted long enough for my chiropractor to buy a new car. I interpreted that as a divine message telling me to stay away from the Presbyterians, at least in a church setting, but there are times, such as this one, when it seems best to be here.

Mike smiles down at me from his place in the choir. I smile back, glad that even after twenty-five years of marriage his smile still brings me pleasure. Mike is one of four paid soloists at this church, and, except for several weeks in the summer, he is here every Thursday night for choir practice and every Sunday morning for two services. It worries me that some of the pap and drivel he hears every Sunday morning might seep in, even though I know that his experience is in the music and not the words, and that he seldom listens to the sermon. And, as the choir rises and fills the building with "And the Glory of the Lord" from Handel's Messiah, I am reminded that the music here is definitely not pap and drivel.

I admit that the church itself looks inviting — hundreds of huge, bright red poinsettias decorate the chancel steps. The dark wooden pews are deeply burnished from decades of polishing and waxing. Plush royal blue cushions pad the seats and plush royal blue carpeting lines the aisles. It is carefully maintained, a beautiful structure, built to the glory of God, but the "no one comes to the father except through the son" is, to me, ridiculous. Nevertheless, here I sit.

I am here this evening because my mother wants to hear Christmas music. Because she wants to hear Mike sing. Because I know it is important for her to get out and to do some of the things she has always done. I'm also here because of guilt and obligation and, let's hope, at least a little bit of love.

A "silent" stroke, drink, age, have all taken their toll on my mother. She has called me several times a day for the past week to remind me that I promised to bring her to this service. Now she is fidgeting.

"Praise God from whom all blessings flow. Praise Her all creatures here below. Praise Her above the heavenly hostess.

Praise mother, daughter and holy ghost-ess."

I sing with conviction, though I am definitely not a singer. Mike's voice, when he decides to use it freely, soars, reaches the highest rafters and the deepest soul. My singing voice is cramped, limited to a range of about five notes, so I can safely shift hymn lyrics to fit my own theological standards without the risk of offending any of the believers around me. I don't want to be offensive; I only want to follow the dictates of "to thine own self be true."

The perpetually tanned doctor-reverend-minister stands before us, arms outstretched, wearing a full flowing, custom tailored, royal blue robe. His theatrically honeyed voice speaks of the babe in the manger — the Christ child. The Christina child, I think, continuing to amuse myself by changing holy genders.

My mother tells me, loudly, that she has to go to the bathroom.

"This should be over in about twenty minutes," I whisper.

"I don't know if I can wait that long," she says.

The woman in front of us turns and throws a frown our way.

"Shall I take you right now?" I ask, again whispering, hoping my mother will take her cue from me and answer back softly.

"No. Pretty soon, though," she says, full voice, checking her watch as if it means something to her.

I look again at the exit sign, calculating the least disturbing way to get my mother from where we are to where she wants to be. It looks different than it did just moments ago. Not only are the letters brighter, the whole sign is bathed in light. It reminds me of the old paintings where Jesus is encompassed in a luminous aura. I feel drawn toward the expanding glow that now floats over the door. At the same time I am inescapably anchored to my mother. Yearning toward a glowing exit sign is new to me. Feeling trapped by my mother's neediness is not.

A roar fills my head, like the roar of an angry sea, or of five o'clock freeway traffic. I close my eyes and listen to inside me — to the roar of why. Why couldn't my mother and I have been soul mates? We are each, in our own way, decent people. If we could ever have gone beyond superficialities, wouldn't it be easier to be patient with her now, in her failing years?

A dizzying turbulence of whispering, whirling noises fills my being and then — another sound, starting low, a growing hum of human voices, instruments, harmonies along a scale of a thousand octaves. I am floating on consonance, elevated a plane above the minister, the choir, my mother, the plush royal blues of carpets and cushions.

"Marilyn," a voice echoes in pure tones.

I nod, keeping my eyes closed, straining to focus on the welling within me.

"Daughter." The voice is rich and resonant, beyond operatic, speaking in chords.

"What??" I whisper, opening my eyes for an instant, seeing as if from a distance the woman who is still checking her watch.

"She, Esther, is your carnal mother. I am your true mother."

Reaching inward for an image to accompany the voice, I catch glimpses of deep purples and reds, flowing silk against an indigo blue.

"Who are you?"

"I am your mother, the Grand Goddess of the Harmonic Universe."

I look around, wondering if anyone else is hearing this conversation. Apparently not. Everyone is looking toward the front where the three wise men have just made their entrance to "Oh, Little Town of Bethlehem." No one seems to have noticed the radiance emanating from the EXIT sign, either. Shit. After all these years of hoping for a religious experience, why does it have to happen in this fundamentalist church? Well, at least it's not Jesus talking to me — not that I have anything against Jesus, I'm just not always wild about the company he keeps.

"I don't get it," I say to my new mother.

"You don't have to get it," the resounding voice answers. "You don't have to have faith, become as a child, or squeeze through the eye of a needle. Here I am. Your true mother. That's all." Then laughter, starting with a chuckle and ending with something of earthquake proportions. I catch sight of my new mother's face. She has green eyes and full lips, emphasized with bright red lipstick. She is wearing blue eye shadow. She has the face of a woman who has been around the block *and* over the hill. Her hair looks bleached.

"Are you cheap?" I ask.

"Honey, I'm not just cheap. I'm free," she bellows.

The image expands. A very big woman, she is floating around, high among the stars of the Pleiades, her rich silken garments wafting gently with the breeze. But would there be a breeze so far out there among the Stars of the Pleiades?

"Don't worry about it," the voice says. "Relax."

With that command, I realize how tense my neck and shoulders are. In the moment of realization my whole body relaxes. A vibrant, pulsing warmth soothes and surrounds me. I see the minister, the choir, the congregation, from a vantage point somewhere near the ceiling, in the center of the building. I see the beauty of the movement of the organist's hands on the keyboard, but I hear music beyond the capabilities of even that glorious instrument. I understand that all the varied people in the congregation are part of a divine oneness.

Poke, poke. Poke, poke. I plunk back down into my body, on the pew next to my carnal mother.

"You'd better take me to the toilet," she says, giving me another poke.

I take her by the arm and guide her as quietly as possible to the door under the radiant EXIT sign. We take baby steps. Mom stops and turns to say something. She can no longer walk and talk at the same time.

"I'm sorry but I guess when you've got to go, you've got to go." She makes a tight little laughing sound.

"It's just around the corner, Mom," I whisper, pressing her on toward the restroom. I open the door to the restroom, and gesture toward one of the stalls. Thank God she can still manage to use the toilet on her own.

"Goddess!" a voice booms in my head.

"Huh?"

"Thank Goddess," is the harmonic response.

"Oh, yeah," I smile.

On the way home the two women say what they always say. How beautifully Mike sang. How wonderful the sermon. Why, you could hear every word he said. He doesn't mumble like some of those young preachers.

As predictable as that all is, there are equally unpredictable things going on. The warmth of another being fills the spaces of the car and encloses me in an ethereal cocoon — not that I can't see the road, or hear my carnal mother and aunt, but I am cushioned by a cloud of . . . what? Peace? Love? Harmony? No. It is something more than can be described by the lyrics from "Hair." Whatever it is, it is deep within me. It encompasses me. It is better than good.

There is a scent, too. A combination of vanilla, licorice and Cherry-A-Let — a long forgotten candy bar, the sudden memory of which causes my mouth to water. Lights and colors are brighter, but at the same time less distinct, as if edges and boundaries have softened. All I can relate this to are stories of drug experiences, or my Aunt Ruth's promise to me that if I would only get saved I would experience the "peace that passeth understanding."

"What's happening?" my inner voice asks.

"Plenty," comes the answer.

"Am I going crazy?"

"Stop with the worrying," bubbles the harmonic laughter.

I take Aunt Hazel home first, then take Mom back to Scripps home and walk her to her room.

"What will I do now?" she asks, wringing her hands.

"Go to bed, probably. It's a little past ten."

"So late?" she whines, then begins her ritual of worries.

"I don't know where my nightgown is. Where will I put my teeth? How will I know when to get up in the morning?"

"It's okay, Mom," I say, showing her the nightgown that is draped across the bed. "I'll get a nurse to come help you get ready for bed."

"But what about in the morning? Can't you stay with me?"

"No, I told Mike I'd meet him at the Ritz-Carlton. I'll phone in the morning."

"But what if the phone isn't working?"

"Then I'll stop by."

One of the aides comes to help Mom get ready for bed and I make my break.

I find Mike near the cocktail lounge. He's sitting on a plush couch in front of a fireplace, sipping wine and eating macadamia nuts. I feel a rush of love as he stands to greet me, kissing me with salty lips.

"How was the music?"

"Wonderful," I say, thinking of the thousand octaved major chords which emanated from beyond the Grand Pleiades.

"How was my solo?"

There was so much going on that I hadn't even noticed Mike's solo, but I'd rather not say so. I'm spared that confession with the waiter's timely appearance.

"Would you care for something to drink? Or something from our bar menu?"

The word Chardonnay is nearly out of my mouth when a harmonic voice suggests a martini.

"I'll have a martini," I say. "Up with an olive."

"A martini?" Mike says, laughing. "Your mother must have pushed you right over the edge tonight."

I consider telling him of my Goddess experience, but maybe I should get to know her better before I introduce Mike to his new mother-in-law.

I caress the smooth roundness of the glass, the delicate rim, then lift it to my lips. What is more refined than a martini glass? I breathe the medicinal scent of gin, which mellows to the Goddess aroma on the next intake. I catch a subtle, reflective glow of purple and red radiating from the translucent glass. We, the three of us, sit in companionable silence while I absorb the beauty and goodness of life into my being.

Monday morning I awaken early. I lie quietly, sensing the warm, soft, big bosomed presence of the Grand Goddess of the Harmonic Universe. Mike stirs. "Um, you're so warm," he says, snuggling. I wonder if the warmth of the goddess is expanding?

When I stop to see Mom on my way home from school on Tuesday, worn from working to impart wisdom to the resistant, I sit in the parking lot for a few minutes, gathering strength. Not that it's an awful place — it's bright and airy, always clean and fresh smelling. There's plenty of activity, and laughter. Still . . . I often have to stare at the trees before I can get out of my car and walk up the steps.

"Let's go," the melodic voice of the universe says.

I get out of the car.

"Do you have a name? Like are you maybe the Christina Child?"

"No way. My mother wasn't a virgin. I'm not a virgin. And I'm not a martyr."

Do the nurses and attendants hear harmonic laughter bouncing from the walls, echoing down the halls? They seem not to.

"Mimi Avocada's my full name, but you can just call me Mimi."

"Who named you?"

"I just came with it. It fits. Sometimes I spell it backwards. You know, the great I M — I M?"

I no longer listen to talk radio when driving. Instead I engage in lengthy conversations with my real mother. Stopped for a red light on my way to school one morning I ask, "What did you think of me as a child?"

"I loved you from the moment of your conception."

"Why didn't you introduce yourself earlier?"

"I was always around, you just didn't recognize me. Sometimes you thought I was someone else."

"Like when? Who did I think you were?"

"What's your earliest dream?"

"I don't know."

"Think about it."

A whirl of purples and reds, scent of vanilla/licorice/Cherry-a-Let; major chords from below sea level to Himalayan peaks mutate to the sound of a loudly blasting horn and I drive on.

That evening, after dinner with Mike, and phone calls to parents of wayward students, and dozing off during the ten o'clock news, I drag myself to bed and think back to Mimi's question about my earliest dream.

In that nearly-asleep-but-not-quite space, it comes to me. It's the dream of Jesus pushing me in a swing — that wonderful, gentle push. I hurl a question out toward the Pleiades.

"What does that dream have to do with you?"

"I told you," comes the booming harmonies. "I was always around, but you didn't recognize me."

"Are you saying you were Jesus?"

"Never! Get it straight. I don't do the martyr thing."

"Well?"

"Well, I'd been watching you. Esther took good care of your bodily needs. That's natural for a carnal mother. But your spirit . . . Remember what she always told you whenever you asked questions about God?"

"Stop bothering me with such silly questions," I say, surprising myself that I still remember feeling hurt over such a long ago slight.

"I thought you needed a lift," Mimi says.

"So why didn't *you* give me one?"

"It wouldn't have meant much right then. I have an in with many symbolic figures. Jesus seemed like a good choice for the time. I knew you'd recognize him."

"You mean you *sent* Jesus?"

"Let's just say we've got sort of a reciprocal agreement going — Jesus, Isis, Buddha, Santa Claus, Mary the Virgin, Kali, Muhammed, the Tooth Fairy."

As I pull into the school parking lot I tell Mimi that I could use some help first period.

"Javier's going to be absent today. First period will be smooth as silk," she says, swirling her garments. "I'm going to hang with the sisters for a while, but remember, "Lo I am with you always, even unto the end."

"Plagiarizing Jesus?" I ask.

"Nope, just another reciprocal agreement," she laughs. Pure tones and full harmonies ease me into the classroom.

Now, nineteen years after the first Mimi appearance she still sometimes glides down from her perch in the Pleiades, bringing peace, and humor and comfort, reminding me that the universe is harmonic.

So . . . what does all this mean? Is Mimi simply a figment of my imagination? If so what purpose does she fulfill? But those are questions that exist in a concrete, literal world. Not that there's anything wrong with that world, but there are other worlds, and Mimi is my means of access to other worlds. I'm grateful for that.

In a recent issue of *The Sun* magazine, I happened on an interview with Krishna Das, an American who is steeped in the practice of "kirtan," an Indian devotional practice that consists of chanting the names of God. Krishna Das says he doesn't even know whether or not he believes in God — "not the one described in Western religious traditions, anyway." He goes on to say:

There are Hindu images associated with God — deities like Krishna, Hnuman, and Kali — but when it comes down to it, these deities are symbols of the divine that lives inside each one of us. Indians are more creative about worship, whereas Christians are generally very tense: there's only one right way to do it and only one God to worship. Of course there is only one God in the Indian traditions, too, just many forms to symbolize it. It's okay to worship anything in any way in India, because there it's understood that nothing is outside of us. There's only one God, and we're all it.

I'm aware that my fundamentalist friends think all of this Mimi stuff is heresy, and that I won't get to heaven if I don't change my way of thinking. But Mimi feels more right to me than any other narrow concept of God to which I've been exposed, so I'm staying with Mimi.

When I, along with so many of my contemporaries, confront the big questions — Is there a god? Will our spirits live on? Will we meet our loved ones on the other side? Will we be judged? — I think of Mimi, the Grand Goddess of the harmonic universe. I think of the love and good will that has come my way throughout my life, in both good times and bad, and I trust that the universe is well-ordered and benign, and that whatever does or does not come after this life is nothing to fear.

A B O U T

T H E

A U T H O R

Marilyn Reynolds is the author of ten books of teen fiction in the popular True-to-Life Series from Hamilton High, and a book for teachers, *I Won't Read and You Can't Make Me: Reaching Reluctant Teen Readers.* In addition to these books for teens and their teachers, Reynolds has numerous personal essays to her credit and was nominated for an Emmy award for the ABC Afterschool Special teleplay of *Too Soon for Jeff.*

Reynolds remains involved in education through author presentations to middle school and high school students ranging from reluctant, struggling readers to highly motivated students who are interested in developing work for possible publication. She also presents training workshops for teachers. In addition to this longtime ongoing work, Reynolds is now writing for her contemporaries and offering writing workshops for the over seventy population — though younger people can also participate. She's not checking I.D.s.

Reynolds lives in Sacramento and enjoys walks along the American River, visits with friends and family, movies and dinners out, and the luxury of reading at odd hours of the day and night.

ORDER FORM
Morning Glory Press
6595 San Haroldo Way, Buena Park, CA 90620-3748
714.828.1998; 1.888.612.8254   Fax 714.828.2049
Or contact Marilyn Reynolds
57 Cadillac Drive, #11, Sacramento, CA 95825
mmreynolds@earthlink.net   www.marilynreynolds.com

		Price	Total
__ Over 70 and I Don't Mean MPH			
ISBN 978-0-9844283-4-2		$12.95	_____

Novels by Marilyn Reynolds:

__ Shut Up!	978-1-932538-88-5	9.95	_____
__ Hardcover	978-1-932538-93-9	15.95	_____
__ No More Sad Goodbyes	978-1-932538-71-7	9.95	_____
__ Hardcover	978-1-932538-72-4	15.95	_____
__ Love Rules	1-885356-76-5	9.95	_____
__ If You Loved Me	1-885356-55-2	9.95	_____
__ Baby Help	1-885356-27-7	8.95	_____
__ Too Soon for Jeff	0-930934-91-1	9.95	_____
__ Detour for Emmy	0-930934-76-8	9.95	_____
__ Telling	1-885356-03-x	9.95	_____

Also by Marilyn Reynolds
__ I Won't Read and You Can't Make Me

	0-325-00605-9	17.00	_____
Add postage: 10% of total—Min., $3.50; 30%, Canada			_____
California residents add 7.75% sales tax			_____
TOTAL			_____

Ask about quantity discounts and Teacher Guides.
Please enclose payment. School/Library purchase orders accepted.

NAME _____ PHONE_____

ADDRESS _____

_____

email _____